RENAISSANCE LEADERSHIP
MANIFESTO

// A POWERFUL GUIDE TO GREATNESS

WITH DEREK GRIER, SAM CHAND, A.R. BERNARD, HARRY JACKSON & CHAPLAIN BARRY BLACK

Renaissance Leadership Manifesto:
A Powerful Guide to Greatness

copyright ©2019

Trade paperback ISBN: 978-1-943294-87-9

Cover design by Martijn van Tilborgh

Published by Renaissance Leadership Network

CONTENTS

INTRODUCTION

//////////////////

I AM HONORED you've chosen to join us on the path towards Godly leadership. As a pastor, I understand firsthand how difficult leadership can be without support from those who understand. My most vibrant and fruitful years as a leader have been fueled by mentorship from business leaders and people of faith who poured into me. My heart is to provide the same thing for you. As you progress in your leadership journey, I want to help encourage you to become all that God has called you to be.

Renaissance Leadership Network's vision is to develop world-class servant leaders devoted to reaching and empowering others. Practically, we accomplish this by training leaders across the country. The Manifesto is part of this initiative.

Church and business leaders face long working hours and carry some of the heaviest burdens in our society. We are often dealing with transitions, working with different people, learning how to steward our gifts, and fostering relationships with God—all at the same time! Leadership is not an easy calling.

We created this Manifesto in order to provide leaders with a field guide for leading with excellence. Inside, you'll find insightful content from a host of influential leaders. Some of my close friends, speakers who have addressed the Renaissance Leadership Network, have contributed their wisdom to this Manifesto. Their firsthand experience will encourage you; their stories and testimonies will inspire you; and their wisdom will improve the way you see and do ministry in your sphere. In these pages, you will find rejuvenation and direction.

My prayer is that, as you are encouraged, you find the strength to encourage others around you, in turn. The Renaissance Leadership Network has impacted thousands of leaders, who in-fluence millions of people around the globe. Our passion is to help leaders unlock their potential, see measurable results, and create a lasting impact.

Above all, know that you are not alone. We are on this path with you. God is beside you in all things, and He will continually bring to fruition His purposes in us, until that day that He comes again to claim us as His own.

Yours in Christ,

Bishop Derek Grier

chapter 1

STRATEGIC PLANNING

//////////////////

by Bishop Derek Grier

For which of you, intending to build a tower, does not sit down first and count the cost, whether he has enough to finish it— lest, after he has laid the foundation, and is not able to finish, all who see it begin to mock him, saying, 'This man began to build and was not able to finish'? —Luke 14:28-30 (NKJV)

THE IMPORTANCE OF PLANNING

HALF-FINISHED STRUCTURES WERE common in the time of Jesus. In a culture obsessed with honor, public failure was embarrassing to the builder and his family. In Luke 14, Jesus is teaching the people that the primary reason for failure, in both our spiritual journeys and our businesses, is a lack of proper planning.

How do we define planning? Alan Lakein notes, "Planning is bringing the future into the present so that you can do something about the future today."[1] Without this forethought, the future simply looms ahead of us—we don't know what course of action to take; and thus, we are less apt to respond well to the circumstances that arise.

Proverbs 21:5 says,

The plans of the diligent lead surely to plenty, but those of everyone who is hasty, surely to poverty.

The adjective "diligent" indicates those individuals who are both thoughtful and industrious—people who don't simply talk about work but who get it done. "The plans of the diligent" are the strategies of people who have planned for the future. This principle is essential for pastors, because hope alone is never an adequate ministry strategy. The reason the devil is gaining ground in our culture today is because Christians have been simply praying, while the "devil kids" have been strategizing. James writes that "faith without works is dead" (James 2:17). It's essential that we don't just believe in our plans—we also have to actively get behind them.

In the New Testament, we see an example of faith and planning coming together. Paul is preparing to receive an offering for the Jerusalem church (see Romans 25 and 1 Corinthians 16 for mention of this offering). Paul meticulously plans for this capital to go to the Jerusalem church: he appoints messengers to come behind him to receive the offering; he makes sure the people handling the offering are those respected within the churches. He coupled faith with developing and working a plan to see the work completed.

So we see that a plan without a goal is just a wish. The way we know we are serious about planning is when we write it down. When we put some elbow grease into developing the strategy.

---

1. *The Art of Personal Effectiveness,* by Eric Garner, Bookboon Publishing, 2012, p. 57.

It's not "plan or pray". It's both working together. Planning is not by any means a bad or unspiritual thing. In fact, it can lead to some of the most fruitful experiences.

How do we approach the future with purpose? After all, the builder in Luke 14 has good intentions; but we see that good intentions, when it comes down to it, are not enough. A good intention with a bad approach still results in a bad outcome. It's easy for us to think, "I heard from God, and my heart is right. Therefore, I am going to do this." Yes, you may have heard from God; but do you know how you're going to do what He's instructed you to do? Our approach matters immensely. The challenge, particularly in the ministry world, is that everyone proclaims that they have great intentions. We need ministry leaders with both the right motivations and strategic ability who can tackle challenges with wisdom.

Jesus, the greatest leader who ever lived, says in Luke 14 that the first thing we have to do is "sit down first and count the cost." The first thing we need in a major venture is some accountability. Accountability is the willingness to answer uncomfortable and important questions. Two such questions that overlap and must be answered early are: what is the mission impact and the profitability of your project?

Let's use Grace Church Daycare as an example. The Grace Church Daycare began with very little. Our mission is to reach, assimilate, empower and lead—primarily, our mission is to share the gospel of Jesus Christ. Everything else is secondary to that purpose. The issue with this learning center was, though it did fall under our vision, it had low mission impact and low profitability. Our prices were low in order to serve people in the community. Over time, we found this posed a problem because the center wasn't highly impacting the mission of the church. We had to make a hard decision, and come to the conclusion that, "Though this fits with our vision, it is not essential. We're going to revisit it, perhaps at another time."

Our TV ministry, in contrast, is high mission impact and low profitability: we're reaching hundreds of thousands of souls a week, but not bringing in a lot of revenue; that ministry is a heart thing for our church, and it's having tangible influence on the people who tune in to it. In this case, we can afford to keep contributing to TV, because we're seeing a yield there.[2]

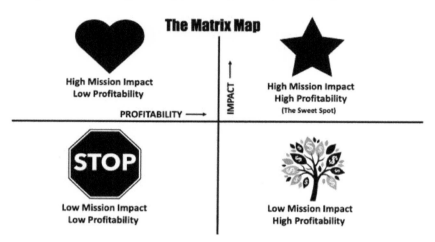

There are also high profitability, low mission impact projects. As Glenn Llopis wrote in Forbes, they are the ones we instinctively gravitate towards.[3] There is a Pastor, for example, whose church also has a learning center. This center didn't impact their mission a lot; however, it proved highly profitable for their church and actually kept them financially afloat during a very difficult season.

God puts certain loves in our hearts. We love some visions, but they don't always add to the ministry's bottom line. The decision you have to make then is, are we seeing enough impact or profitability to justify keeping this initiative in the strategic plan?

2. *NPQ – Non Profit Quarterly,* "The Matrix Map: A Powerful Tool for Mission-Focused Nonprofits," by Steve Zimmerman and Jeanne Bell, April 1, 2014

3. *https://www.forbes.com/sites/glennllopis/2014/01/13/8-qualities-thatmake-leaders-extraordinarily-memorable/#5f1a92407565*

The bullseye is when you hit a place where you have high mission and high profitability. This is where you want to be. The keyword in all of this planning is sustainability. It's easy to start something; it's another thing to keep it going. Let's look at another example.

Consider McDonald's. Their bread and butter, you could say, is their burgers and fries. If push came to shove, and something happened financially where their kitchen could no longer afford to produce both burgers and chicken nuggets, guess what they would have to do? They would be forced to choose to eliminate the nuggets to keep the burgers and fries on the menu. In the same way, in ministry, we've got to keep our main thing—sometimes, this results in making some tough decisions. Not everyone is going to approve or to like these calls—people may get mad at you or your team. This is why you need good representatives to come alongside you and communicate your strategic plan.

In the church, we have to teach the gospel. If we get so busy with other things that we can't do that, we are in trouble. For us, everything else is secondary to that primary piece.

QUESTIONS TO GET YOU STARTED

Part of what a strategic plan does is that it takes you through the discipline of knowing what your main thing is, and then making certain that thing continues. In the language of McDonald's, if we know what our "main dish" and "side dishes" are, we can keep those priorities in place. I've adapted five questions from Peter Drucker, a business thinker who had a great influence on me and the business world at large. It will help you begin meaningful conversations with your leadership team. Take a moment to reflect and write your thoughts on each of these.

1. What is your business? What's the main thing—your mission, core values, what you provide to the community? This may be your church's unique phrasing of the Great Commission

or the gospel message. Articulate your why so that you have a foundation off of which to build everything else.

2. What would your business, church, or department become if it continues as is? What would happen to it— what would it look like—five years down the line if nothing at all changed? Would you be where you want to be? It's important to take an honest look at the practices we are currently enacting. The first step to change is being up front about where we're currently positioned.

3. What should your business, church or department become? This question often leads to the tough conversations—often, our current course of action and our ultimate vision are not congruent, as stated in the last question. What is it that you need to modify—how will you adjust course? Make these assessments and acknowledge the resulting decisions that your team faces.

4. Which of your present businesses, ministries and departments should you prune to ensure that you become what you must? This question incorporates findings from the hard conversations that executives must have. If you want to adjust your trajectory, you have to take some sort of action. Consult with your team and commit to making the changes necessary to sustaining your mission.

5. Which business, ministry, department, or product should you push and contribute to with your resources? Determine what you will focus on moving forward. Will you contribute more funding to a certain ministry? Will your team focus on a specific theme or Biblical principle in the next season? This may be where some exciting op-portunities come to light in your conversations.

The builder in Luke 14 ended up embarrassed because he didn't ask himself the right questions. If we narrow these questions down to one that will help you create a strategic plan, it's this:

What do I have to do now to obtain what I want tomorrow?

At some point, we need to give up what has been to become all that God has called us to be. That's the difficult part, because we're comfortable and familiar with what has been; but sometimes, we've got to let go of that to step into what God has called us to do.

Proverbs 16:3 says, "Commit to the Lord whatever you do, and he will establish your plans." If you don't have plans, though, God has nothing to establish.

At the same time we know that we don't always get it right. I've heard stories of folks that were part of the early journeys to the moon. While we can tend to assume that they just climbed into a rocket and shot to the moon on the first attempt, that's not what happened at all. On that first suc-cessful voyage, the astronauts were constantly in touch with mission control down on earth. Every ten minutes, or so, they had to adjust course. They would get a call from NASA, who'd say, "You need to adjust by 5° due east." Just like that, there are going to be course corrections we need to make on our journeys. That's why we have to stay prayed up with our Mission Control: ask the Lord consistently whether you should take that next step. Listen to Him, and make course corrections on your journey. He will never steer you off course.

WHAT A STRATEGIC PLAN IS NOT[4]

We also don't want to overcomplicate things. Let's discuss what a strategic plan is not.

1. Strategic planning is not forecasting the future. Only God knows the future—every now and then, he gives us a peek. Strategic planning is simply taking the next steps to continue your current vision into the tomorrow.

---

4. The following information was adapted from *Management: Tasks, Responsibilities, Practices,* by Peter Drucker, Harper Collins, 1974.

2. Strategic planning does not deal with future decisions. It deals with the futurity of present decisions. It's asking 'How is this decision today going to impact our future? What are we willing to do now to obtain our ob-jectives tomorrow?"

3. Strategic planning is not an attempt to eliminate risk, but helps us prepare for the risks that lie ahead. Faith is alternatively spelled R-I-S-K. We will never get it so mapped out that there's no risk. There's always going to be risk involved. However, we can begin to manage risk through a strategic plan.

A SIMPLE TEMPLATE FOR A STRATEGIC PLAN

Sometimes, we make the planning process too complicated. At its essence, planning is about getting from Point A to Point B. Believe it or not, this can be pleasant! Plans can be as simple as a three-page document, or as in-depth as a fifty-page document. It all depends on your organization's needs.

Let's walk through a simple example of a strategic plan.

The first portion of the plan is outlining the following for your organization: your mission, core values, competitive advantage, and strategy. Let's examine each of these in detail.

Mission

It's important that you articulate your mission. Make sure that this statement is concise and concrete. You don't want a rambling manifesto—just one with the power to guide your activities.

Core Values

Your core values should answer the question, "How do we want to behave?" Before you develop strategies, you must know what the operating principles are: how will you and your team behave, or operate, as you execute those strategies?

Competitive Advantage

A good way to phrase this piece is by asking yourself the question, "How will we win?" What's the element of your business that makes it unique? What can you capitalize on to bring your vision to life? Here at Grace Church, we will win by maintaining and adhering to our core values.

Strategies

This, finally, answers the question, "How will we play?" If you keep your core values in mind as you develop strategies, you will be successful. This is where the above values find practical application in your organization. Once you have all four of these elements, you are ready to structure measures of success into your plan. How will you be able to judge whether you're being successful and staying on track? The following are some practical tips to ensuring your plan is effective:

1. Identify individuals who will execute your strategies. Write a name next to that task, and give that person a timeline (i.e. "By the second quarter of 2018, we're going to broaden our campaign. Anna will be working on this strategy and will have specific, smaller strategies in place in order to reach that goal"). This ensures the items don't fall through the cracks in the weeks to come.

2. Keep track of metrics to discern growth. For churches, tracking things such as weekly attendance, and the factors that influence it, will give your team an understanding of how your strategy is playing out practically. Then, you can adjust things as needed. Identify key performance indicators (KPIs) that will communicate the success of your strategies. Look for things you don't know or would like more information on, and then create metrics to give you answers to those gray areas. Data spreadsheets may not be flashy, but they're extremely helpful when you need insight into your current course of action. Another note: make sure these metrics measure things that truly matter. You can measure the people who walk in the door, but are those people truly engaged? A better metric to your success might be how many of those people are serving in the church on a regular basis.

3. Be accountable. What will stop your team from putting your plan on a shelf and not looking at it again until next year? You must have that accountability we touched on earlier. Whether this takes shape in the form of quarterly reviews, mid-year planning retreats, external stakeholder reviews, or other tools, make sure your plan is truly a living document. We recommend quarterly and annual regroups with your team to establish a unified mindset and evaluate your progress.

Additionally, make sure a variety of position levels and age groups are present at these meetings, as much as possible. These varying perspectives will benefit the conversation and help individuals at all levels of your team feel involved in the process.

In summary, consider where you want to go, and how you want to get there. Brainstorm some fun things that you can do to engage your team, as well as help them understand the business and their roles in it.

THE SWOT METHOD[5]

One more tool you can use in your strategic planning is the SWOT method. SWOT stands for Strengths, Weaknesses, Opportunities, and Threats. This filter works well when analyzing the effectiveness of long-term goals. Here's how each part breaks down:

Strengths

Strengths focus on internal factors: What do you do well? What unique resources can you draw on in your organization? How do you differentiate yourself from your competition?

Weaknesses

What can you improve? What are others saying about your organization and how it can improve? See this not as a condemning exercise but as opportunity to increase your effectiveness by listening to feedback.

---

5. *https://www.edenscott.com/blog/how-to-do-your-own-swot-analysis*

Opportunities

These tend to center on external factors. What current trends can you take advantage of for your organization? What clues are certain demographics giving you about what resources you can utilize? What are other organizations taking advantage of that could also benefit your organization?

Threats

Threats are things that could harm you. What, for instance, is your competition doing? How could your weaknesses expose you to threats? Discerning threats is integral to wisely facing the challenges in your future. You have to be prepared before you go into battle.

When looking at the SWOT method, again, it's important to be honest with yourself. Some companies make this evaluation interactive, writing the categories in visible spaces and giving participants sticky notes to add to each section. Then, as a group, they'll discuss what needs to be addressed, and in what order. Once people are engaged, the process is easier and includes many perspectives.

WHEN A PLAN IS NOT SUSTAINABLE

What do we do when we discover a plan we are not able to finish, like the man in Luke 14? Is it better to simply let that idea go? Should we try to salvage it if possible?

Maybe. It all depends on your unique situation. This goes back to the central principle of sustainability. Some things may be feasible in a seasonal sense (going back to McDonald's, think about the McRib—they may not be able to serve it year-round, but every year when it does become a feature again, people get excited and the demand is there). Alternatively, if you're a business, you may have the option to sell a part or the whole to someone else and make a profit. Or, you may be able to hand your venture to someone else who does have the means to continue it.

RENAISSANCE LEADERSHIP MANIFESTO

There are a multitude of options available. If you adjust your thinking, a creative solution will arise. The important thing is to be honest in discerning and admitting that there are some plans you will not be able to sustain.

CLOSING THOUGHTS

The world is planning. As believers, we have the strategic opportunity to plan and to pray, which gives us a huge advantage. However, if we only pray, we will soon be left behind. That being said, be sure to choose your battles wisely—no one can do everything at once. Choose one thing to focus on at a time, and then proceed to the next thing. Use the tools we discussed in a way that renders them helpful and a blessing you and your organization. May God make Himself and His will known as you strategically plan for your future, and may you involve Him intimately in the process.

Dr. Derek Grier is the founding pastor of Grace Church in Dumfries, Virginia. He was ordained as a bishop in 2008, and earned a Master's in Education from Regent University and a Doctorate in Practical Ministry from Wagner University. Dr Grier has authored several books, and leads programs specializing in education, training, and outreach. Derek and his wife, Yeromitou, live in northern Virginia and have two adult sons.

chapter 2

HOW TO STEWARD AND RELEASE YOUR GIFT TO THE MARKET

/////////////////

by Martijn van Tilborgh

I CAME TO THIS COUNTRY IN 2006. Before then, I had been involved in full-time church planning work in South Africa and the Netherlands. Ministry was my life. I thought that's what I would do the rest of my life.

Then, God began opening doors for me in the United States, and I realized he was sending me there. My wife and I had no idea what we would do in America; after all, I believed I was living the life I was supposed to live up until that point. Then, three things happened. My finances dried up. My net worth got damaged. Doors that had been open were no longer open. The ministry I was involved in imploded overnight. There I was, lying in bed in 2008, and I said, "Lord, I am $60,000 in debt. The ministry I thought I had no longer exists. I have no clue what to do. What is it that you want me to do? Now what?"

He showed me a vision of the disciples walking with Jesus. I imagine they thought they were living the life—doing what they were born to do. Then, Jesus sits them down and says, "Guess what, guys? It's to your advantage that this stops." Why? Because Jesus had something for them that was far greater than what they were currently experiencing.

One of the principles of the kingdom is the law of death and resurrection—everything must die first, and then it can be resurrected. We all want to experience God's resurrection power, but we don't want to experience death. I realized the Lord Himself was killing my ministry. I said, "Lord, you killed me, and You resurrect me...but what is it I'm supposed to do?"

So, in 2008, I picked up the classified ads and started calling local businesses. One of the first businesses I talked to was Lake Mary Mini Storage. I sold them a website I didn't know how to build for $299. Then I did an online course. Then I built a website for $299. That's how I started. In four months, I was where I wanted to be, and in eight months, we had doubled that. A year later, we doubled it again, and so on until we reached the point where we were making millions.

In that journey, I discovered a few things I think will help you in your organization or ministry.

INFLUENCE → DATABASE → ENGAGEMENT → DOLLARS

I see many ministries pouring money into things that don't contribute to their bottom line: "fancy billboards in the desert," we call them. They look pretty, but nobody looks at them for very long. I become interested in the psychology of what keeps people engaged long enough for me to tell my story. Here's what I found.

When people come to a website, they ask three questions; if you're not answering these questions, they will not be satisfied, and will move on from your site.

1. Where am I?

2. What can I do here?

3. Why should I do that with you?

Even in ministry, we must discuss a bottom line. A bottom line has to do with the objective of why you have your web presence in the first place; it can be a nonprofit cause, but you still want people to answer your call to action. There's still a result you're pursuing. A bottom line moves us forward towards that result.

How do we get where we want to be? Firstly, we need to identify our platforms of influence.

Platforms of Influence

Your platforms of influence can be online or offline. They include, but are not limited to: your website, your social media, your TV or radio ministry, your Sunday or Wednesday church services, your community events, and so on. Wherever there is influence, we can put mechanisms in place to convert these platforms into a database.

Databases

How can I further the conversation after my audience "leaves"? I can only do this if I know who they are—if I assimilate data. In building websites, I became skilled at database-building audience developments: we converted data into a landing page outside of the normal web presence. This resulted in a 70-80% conversion rate from the old traffic to the new database. All this to say, we created a space for those audiences to engage with us. This is the next element.

Engagement

Without engagement, there's nothing to launch from in your ministry or business. Any product, service, or ministry must be launched off engagement. This is where you generate an appetite for what you have by showing people that they will benefit from it—that you have created value. This leads to the final element...

Dollars

Once you have engagement and that appetite, you can convert that into dollars, or whatever it is you're trying to convert it into. People will pay for the value that you possess, whether that's in a product, a talk, or a service.

When people ask me, "What do you do?" this is it: I turn influence into dollars.

SHEPHERDS IN THE WILDERNESS

I've come full circle. I knew that I came to this country with a purpose, but it ended up looking much different than I thought it would. In reflecting on this, God showed me a truth about living the abundant life He promises us. Jesus says in John 10:10,

> *"The thief does not come except to steal, and to kill, and to destroy. I have come that they may have life, and that they may have it more abundantly." —John 10:10 (NKJV)*

What do we usually think about when we read about the thief's destruction? Maybe it's poverty, sickness, death, strife, jealousy... these are obvious things the enemy deploys to destroy us. But one day, I was reading this scripture, and the Lord said to me, "Could it be that the most powerful way the thief comes to destroy is by making you believe that the life you live today is, in fact, the abundance Jesus has for you, while in reality there's a world out there you don't even know exists that is the true abundance you're looking for?" I thought, if this is true, wouldn't we want to enter that world at any cost? Like the disciples, I realized I had been living m life and not seeing the advantages Jesus has in store through a path different than the one I was currently walking.

Here's another story to illustrate this idea. In Zechariah 2, there's an account of a man with a measuring rod:

> *Then I raised my eyes and looked, and behold, a man with a measuring line in his hand. So I said, "Where are you going?"*

And he said to me, "To measure Jerusalem, to see what is its width and what is its length."

And there was the angel who talked with me, going out; and another angel was coming out to meet him, who said to him, "Run, speak to this young man, saying: 'Jerusalem shall be inhabited as towns without walls, because of the multitude of men and livestock in it. For I,' says the Lord, 'will be a wall of fire all around her, and I will be the glory in her midst.'"
—Zechariah 2:1-5 (NKJV)

The man with the measuring line is similar to you and me: full of the zeal of the Lord, wanting to do the right thing. He thinks, "I'm going to build the city of God!" He thinks he's doing all the right stuff, and then the angel stops him. He says, "Where do you think you're going?"

"I'm building Jerusalem!" the man says.

The angel says, "Wait. Actually, Jerusalem will be inhabited as towns without walls and, I, the Lord, will be a wall of fire all around them." There was a huge misconception the man had—that the city would have walls—and therefore he was taking with him the tools he assumed were the correct ones needed to build the city.

Think about these tools: the measuring rod is a standard created by whom? Man. Somebody decided, back in history, "This is a meter," and from then on everything was measured by this standard. Let me ask you this: How many "measuring rods" do we have in our thinking that have become assumptions on how we are to do the Lord's work? Could it be that we're controlled by a mindset of limitation that creates the illusion that *this is all there is*?

In Revelation, we read about the door in heaven opening; a voice comes out of the door and says: *"John, come up here so I can show you what must take place after this."* What stands out to me about this command is that there had to be an *elevation* of what John could see before he could move into his next season. I've come to believe that, just like the Israelites who were sentenced to die in the wilderness for their lack of belief, many of us have become shepherds in the wilderness. God led the Israelites to the Promised Land, but because they doubted, they were relegated to become something they were never meant to be for forty years. When you spend long enough being something you were never meant to be, you stop questioning it.

Could it be that the Church has become shepherds in the wilderness—in an exile where we all act the same, do ministry the same way, and do business the same way? And, if so, how do we dismantle that mindset of limitation in a practical way? How do we steward our God-given talents well, and move into the greater world he has for us?

STEWARDING AND RELEASING YOUR GIFT

Stewardship over talent has two dimensions. First of all, the talent: your gift. God gives unique skills to every individual. Secondly, we also steward the monetary aspect of what that gift entails. In the Parable of the Talents, good stewardship led to monetary talents multiplied. If you steward them well, your message and your finances, have the ability to travel further, leaving a higher impact on more people.

In business terms, branding, advertising, and marketing have everything to do with your story and your value. A lot of ministries don't capitalize on their story, but it's essential: it's the communication of that unique element God has given to you and only you.

Isaiah 43:19 says,

Behold, I will do a new thing,
Now it shall spring forth;
Shall you not know it?
I will even make a road in the wilderness
And rivers in the desert. (NKJV)

We can run the risk of making this a mystical revelation about an unknown thing. However, if you're created by divine design, that means there's only one you. What you bring to the table is absolutely unique, by definition. There's a lot you can do with the body of Christ, but part of our journey is the development into that something where nobody else can quite help you.

Let's look at an example of this in Matthew 16:13-20. Peter and Jesus are having a conversation. Jesus asks him, "Who do the people say I am?" Peter more or less answers, "Some say you're John. Some say you're one of the prophets. Some say you're crazy. The word on the street is very diverse."

"Alright," Jesus says, "Thank you. Now I know what other people say about me, but who do you say that I am?

"You're the Christ, the Son of the living God.

Then what does Jesus say? "Wow. I never told you that. This is concealed revelation in this time period. You couldn't have known that unless you had a supernatural experience with God that showed you something about me that nobody else knows. And on his rock I will build my church." This level of revelation becomes a foundation on which the church is built. And then he continues. "And the gates of hell cannot prevail against that."

We need God to pinpoint our gifts. We need to take a hold of them. We need to have a revelation of who we are before we can overcome the gates of hell—or reorganize our ministries. Your gift comes exclusively out of your relationship with God. Once He's revealed it to you, you can move on to sharing that gift with your market.

YOUR MARKET: INCENTIVE AND THE "FUNNELING" METHOD

Who constitutes your market? This can be answered by asking this question: who can most benefit from your gift, and where do you find those people? That's your market. What keeps us from effectively releasing our gift to the market? The answer is lack of innovation. We like to say, "There's no competition in the kingdom. We're all brothers and sisters." However, we only say that until somebody opens a church next door to ours. The truth is that the Kingdom is the unique expression of every individual—God's manifold wisdom. In Dutch, the translation of the word "manifold" is many colors: the spectrum of the many colors of God. Somewhere in that spectrum I'm there. You're there, too. So, in releasing and marketing our gifts, we optimize where we can, but we also innovate by digging deep into *who God wants you to be.*

I was in San Antonio not too long ago; there's a historical invention that was created there. Can you guess what it was? Barbed wire. Why is barbed wire so significant? Because up until it was invented, people would have to wake up in the morning, put on their hunting gear, go into the wilderness, shoot something, bring it home, and cook a meal. That translates to a lot of energy expended with pretty short term benefit. Then, barbed wire was invented. People started to corral cattle together. Now, all they needed to do was roll out of bed and pick the cattle they wanted from the pen for that day's meals. That's good stewardship: working smarter, not harder.

How can we create an environment like that—one where we contain our prospects? I've discovered it's possible. It's called developing engagement. Let me share an example of how this works.

We did an online event with Sam Chand, who was releasing his book. We gave away 4,500 books while generating a half a million-dollar revenue. Thomas Nelson is still confused about how it happened. When most people advertise, they have this line of communication that says: "Our products are amazing. You should buy them." This isn't effective, though, because I have to take your word for it, and I don't know you from Adam. A better marketing strategy sounds like this: "Man, I've been sitting in on the Bishop's ministry for the last two years. This is what it did for me. It's amazing. You should listen to him, too."

This adds third-party credibility to the message. But you still have to take my word for it. Maybe he's paying me, after all.

What we ultimately want is called inception. Maybe you've seen the movie by the same title. The premise is that we can plant ideas in people's minds through a dream. They wake up and believe the thought is theirs. Like every sales process, this delves into psychology; there's nothing wrong with utilizing psychology; but with great power comes great responsibility. I've learned to use this for good—if God has something to give to an audience, I am not afraid to use psychology to get it to them. Inception is an exchange I create with my prospect wherein he gets to experience the value I have, and thinks it is his or her idea to buy from me. Instead of chasing them, they start chasing me.

There are two kinds of people in this world: people who run from pain and people who run towards pleasure. Most people fall into the former category. If we're in leadership, we understand that people in every organization struggle with pain—some have depression, anxiety, or even suicidal thoughts. If I can show those people a thriving organization where the employees are healthy, and indicate that I can move them from where they are to this finish line, with evidence, guess what? They are going to pay for it. If I can enter their world and show them that I understand what they're going through, and answer questions they've been asking themselves, I've added value. Then, they desire more: they ask me, "What else have you got?"

This process doesn't come to fruition overnight. You build it. I've sold products before that took about two months to build—I'd be giving, giving, giving. Then, at some point, I tell people I am going to ask for something, so they're mentally prepared; but by that point, I've created a system wherein everybody's going to want what I am offering and are going to give me what I ask for. This ladder always begins with the free engagement.

THE TARGET

What are your marketing efforts aiming towards? What is it that you're trying to accomplish? At the end of the day, while marketing Sam Chand's book, we recognized that it wasn't about the book. It was about the message—maximizing the audience reached. The book was just the vehicle. So, we evaluated our products and reverse-engineered the process—in other words, we didn't start with the $1,600 product; instead, we invited people to a free event during which we gave away books. Then we said, "If you really want to benefit from this book, will you take a five-week journey with me? I'll break down the message for you, make it practical." I added a five-week master class to the funnel cycle. Then I said, "If you're enrolling in the master class, chances are you're a leader. Why not have your whole team do the course? Check this box and you can share it with your team." That's the funnel method. You offer the audience opportunities, but only if they first take advantage of your previous offerings: "You don't get *this* unless you first get *this*."

A quick principle to write down: if you cannot give a product away for free, people probably won't want to pay for it. That's why a funnel starts with the free, and then moves people down the sales cycle.

YOUR TURN

In discussing marketing and releasing your gift to the market, it all comes down to this: rely on God to reveal what your unique gift is; steward it well by working smart and multiplying what you've been given; and demonstrate that your product solves people's problems. It can work with any product: information, vitamins, online church—the list goes on. You may have to be patient, but these principles will start to change things for your organization—what you have will begin to multiply.

I started out with nothing; I only had the classified ads, a phone, and an online course. Looking back, it's incredible how

God multiplied my influence. Put your trust in Him, and steward what He's given you well; He will multiply what you have for His purposes.

Martijn van Tilborgh is a marketing architect, speaker, author, and serial entrepreneur. He consults with countless large organizations and has launched many of his own products. Martijn is always looking to create the next big thing in the different niches he works in. He, his wife Amy, and his three children reside in Orlando, Florida.

chapter 3

HOW TO BE A GREAT LEADER

/////////////////

by Pastor Van Moody

I HAVE A GREAT PASSION for pouring into leaders. I believe the kingdom of God rises and falls on great leaders. I also believe we are called to do business. Jesus tells His disciples to occupy their roles until He comes again: the word "occupy" literally means to do business. So you could say that the disciples were entrepreneurs. Out of all the people He could have chosen, Jesus approaches this group of men who hadn't been smart enough to pass their rabbinical tests and therefore were working in their families' businesses. What's the lesson here? The calling God has on your life, no matter what it is, is significant. When we in the Church raise up more kingdom leaders with integrity, we're going to see God work in a great way.

THE CENTRALITY OF RELATIONSHIPS

If I could sum up leadership in one word, it would be relationships. It doesn't matter whether your sphere of influence is big or small—relationships are the key. Christianity is also about relationships. How many of you remember the man who runs up to Jesus and asks, "Of all the law of Moses, which is the greatest commandment?" Jesus answers,

> *"'You shall love the Lord your God with all your heart, with all your soul, and with all your mind.' This is the first and great commandment. And the second is like it: 'You shall love your neighbor as yourself.' On these two commandments hang all the Law and the Prophets." — Matthew 22:37-40 (NKJV)*

When Jesus says "all the law and the prophets," He's saying, "I can sum up the Old Testament with this statement." Later on in the book of John, Jesus says,

> *By this all will know that you are My disciples, if you have love for one another." —John 13:35 (NKJV)*

Jesus says the identifying marker of a true disciple is how he or she handles relationships. Everywhere Jesus went, people followed Him. Why? Because He made people His passion. Jesus touched them not just spiritually, but physically, emotionally, mentally, because He was a great leader. If you cannot relate well with people, you will not be able to lead your organization, business, or ministry effectively. Success, for great leaders, is when other people win, and when they as a leader win with those people.

PEOPLE AND LEADERS

I want to give you some nuggets to sink your teeth into as we unpack this notion of leadership and relationships. Here are four truths about people and leaders.

1. *People are an organization's greatest asset.* It doesn't matter how great your idea is; people are your greatest asset. If you handle people well, they will be the greatest blessing to your organization; if you mismanage them, they will become the greatest burden.

2. *A leader's most important asset is his or her people skills.* One of the greatest attributes a leader can possess is the ability to work well with people.

3. *A good leader can lead various groups.* I have traveled around the world and shared with a number of leaders. There are some who say things like, "My business didn't work out because I was in the wrong sector," or, "I had a problem in my church because my spirit didn't bear witness with those kinds of people." These leaders mistakenly believe the problems lie within these other spheres, when in reality, they simply don't work well with other people. When you can relate well with others, you can be in any place, in any sector, doing anything, and rock it.

4. *You can have people skills and not be a good leader.* I know some who have great people skills, but not a calling for leadership. I also know great leaders who are horrible with people, and they're not as great as they could be.

The way you see yourself impacts the way you lead. I think it was Leo Tolstoy who said that the greatest war you will ever fight is the one raging inside of you. Many times, leaders have been shaped by negative experiences; when these experiences aren't processed well, they can end up duplicating what was done to them. Jesus deals with this principle in the parable of the Good Samaritan.

And behold, a certain lawyer stood up and tested Him, saying, "Teacher, what shall I do to inherit eternal life?"

He said to him, "What is written in the law? What is your reading of it?"

So he answered and said, "'You shall love the Lord your God with all your heart, with all your soul, with all your strength, and with all your mind,' and 'your neighbor as yourself.'"

And He said to him, "You have answered rightly; do this and you will live."

RENAISSANCE LEADERSHIP MANIFESTO

But he, wanting to justify himself, said to Jesus, "And who is my neighbor?"

Then Jesus answered and said: "A certain man went down from Jerusalem to Jericho, and fell among thieves, who stripped him of his clothing, wounded him, and departed, leaving him half dead. Now by chance a certain priest came down that road. And when he saw him, he passed by on the other side. Likewise a Levite, when he arrived at the place, came and looked, and passed by on the other side. But a certain Samaritan, as he journeyed, came where he was. And when he saw him, he had compassion. So he went to him and bandaged his wounds, pouring on oil and wine; and he set him on his own animal, brought him to an inn, and took care of him. On the next day, when he departed, he took out two denarii, gave them to the innkeeper, and said to him, 'Take care of him; and whatever more you spend, when I come again, I will repay you.' So which of these three do you think was neighbor to him who fell among the thieves?"

And he said, "He who showed mercy on him."

Then Jesus said to him, "Go and do likewise." —Luke 10:25-37 (NKJV)

One of the teachers of the law comes to Jesus and says, "Well, who is my neighbor?" He's trying to skirt around the reality that leadership is about people. In response, Jesus tells this parable. He asks the man in the end, "Who do you think was the greatest neighbor?" Begrudgingly the guy says, "The Samaritan," and then storms off.

It's more than just a spiritual parable. It's a parable about leadership. Your ministry is not confined to your current sphere of influence. The priest and Levites said, "He's unclean, so let us walk around him." No. As a leader, your sphere can never be confined to the people you're comfortable with. Every person you come into contact with holds the potential for the thing that God as birthed in you.

There are three main characters in the parable of the Good Samaritan. They seem themselves in different ways and thus, live differently. First, there are the robbers, or thieves. They manipulated people, so saw the man as a victim to exploit. The priests, who considered themselves pure in society, saw a problem to avoid—an impurity. Lastly, there is the Samaritan. This man knew how it felt to be ignored and despised; when he saw the injured man, he saw him as a person to be loved.

As a leader, you will be tempted to exploit and avoid people. My prayer for you, though, is that you love people. The goal is to look past their faults, see their potential, and see their needs. A great leader is one who assumes responsibility for the health and development of their relationships. People are not going to follow you simply because of your title or position. The number one responsibility of any leader in any position is to develop relational equity with the people you've got to lead.

THE PORTRAIT OF A GREAT LEADER

Let me give you four word pictures that illustrate relational equity. These illustrations demonstrate how to build relational equity with people.

The Host

When you host people at your home, first of all, you're going to clean your house. You're going to make sure the house looks presentable when they show up. You've got the cheese platter or whatever it is that you lay out. You've cultivated an environment for people to feel comfortable. Then when they show up, you're going to answer the door, right? You're going to smile. Preferably, you've washed up and you smell good. You're going to warmly welcome them into your space, but then you're not just going to say, "Okay, just do whatever you're going to do." No, because they've never been to your home before.

You're going to show them around and say, "Here's this room, and if you need anything, let me know." That's what a good host does, right? How many of you have been to good restaurants where you've been ignored by the host? What do you say? "Not coming back here," because the host defines the experience. As a leader, you have to host the relationships in your life— the conversations in your sphere of influence. You're not the "guest" in the relationship.

The Doctor

All of us have been to a good doctor—what do they do? They're going to ask questions. "How do you feel? What's going on? Anything bothering you?" They're going to look in your ear, use that tongue depressor, ask you to say "Ah..." They're going to get an understanding of the diagnosis before they write a prescription.

As a leader, the worst thing you can do is prescribe a remedy without a good understanding of the diagnosis. There are so many leaders who jump to conclusions: "Oh, let me tell you what you need." No, you don't know what I need, because you haven't asked the questions. You've got to do the work. Only then can you address needs. Don't ever try to give a prescription before you've got the diagnosis.

The Counselor

Counselors are active listeners. If you've ever been to counseling and sat on that couch, it's all about you. The counselor never says, "I've been waiting for you to get here: there's so much I want to tell you." No, the counselor gets comfortable, and for the majority of that session, they're going to listen. They may ask a couple questions, but you do the majority of the talking. As a leader, you've got to be an active listener, which includes your verbal and nonverbal responses. You earn the right to speak, then, because you build relational equity.

The Tour Guide

There is a difference between a travel agent and a tour guide. I got a chance to meet Bishop and Pastor Grier when we were traveling with a mutual friend, Dr. Sam Chand, in Panama. It was a small group of leaders that gathered to fellowship and learn; Dr. Chand's team functioned as our tour guides—we didn't have to worry about anything along the journey. When we landed, for instance, we were escorted from the plane through immigration. While a travel agent can book the ticket and tell you where to go, a tour guide is going to be on the ground, walking with you every step of the way. As leaders, we're called to be tour guides. This isn't about always being liked; it's about casting the vision of the church and then walking alongside the people you lead in that journey.

STRUGGLES OF LEADERSHIP

In order to be an effective leader, you've got to have space for honest analysis of the people you're leading. Ephesians 4:29 says,

> *Do not let any unwholesome talk come out of your mouths, but only what is helpful for building others up according to their needs, that it may benefit those who listen.*

This is absolutely true; and yet, I want to get to the heart of the issues we face as leaders. Here are ten principles every leader should keep in mind about people.

1. *People are insecure: give them confidence.* Hurt people hurt people; secure people offer security to other people. Insecure leaders will try to gain security from people instead of giving it. A secure environment can only be provided by secure leaders. Remember, success for a great leader is other people winning. Leaders are other-focused. You cannot be other-focused if there's still a deficit in you.

2. *People like to feel special: honor them.* This is essential. People need honor. When I teach on marriage, one of the things I love sharing with wives is that men are all insecure in some way. One of the greatest things a wife can do for a husband is to honor him where she wants him to be, not where he is. The same applies in leadership. Honor

people where you want them to be; they will rise to that occasion. If you demean them, they're going to shrivel.

3. *People look for a better tomorrow: give them hope.* Whether you know it or not, as a leader, you're a dealer in hope. We traffic in hope. This is why God puts Ezekiel in the valley of dry bones and raises a question.

And He said to me, "Son of man, can these bones live?"

So I answered, "O Lord God, You know."

Again He said to me, "Prophesy to these bones, and say to them, 'O dry bones, hear the word of the Lord! —Ezekiel 37:3-4 (NKJV)

God wants us to speak those things that are not as though they are. One of the greatest keys you have is a vision for what's beyond. People look for a better tomorrow, so give them hope. Your constant communication ought to be about where your congregation can be. You ought to be in love with the vision God has given you. If not, once discouragement settles in, you'll walk away. You've got to be in love with it, and that ought to be at the heart of what you communicate.

4. *People need to be understood: listen to them.*[6] Great leaders seek first to understand and then be understood. What did they talk about? What did they cry about? What have they dreamed about? When you know what they're dreaming about, you can help them connect their dream to your dream. People need to be needed and known. One of the ways you prove they are needed is by understanding how their dream connects with the bigger picture of the dream God has given you.

5. *People like direction: navigate for them.* A lot of people can steer the ship, but great leaders chart the course.

---

6. *https://www.franklincovey.com/the-7-habits/habit-5.html*

Many leaders are master delegators; and while you do need to be able to delegate, you cannot delegate charting the course of where the organization is going. As John Maxwell writes, "Leaders must know the way, go the way, and show the way."[7] You've got to do all three.

6. *People are needy: speak to their needs first.* People must be ministered to before they will minister. Do you know the needs of the people in your organization? Have you met them? If not, there's your first step.

7. *People get emotionally low, so encourage them.* One of the greatest things you can do is traffic in encouragement. There was an experiment done years ago to find out how long a person could stand in a bucket of ice water. For the first test group, they simply told them, "Take your shoes off and stand in there." They timed how long the individuals could do so. In the second group, they had people around to encourage them: "Come on! You can do it! Hang in there! One more minute!" Guess which participants lasted the longest in the bucket? The second group. That's the power of encouragement.

8. *People want to succeed: help them win.* You'll be surprised how quickly morality rises in your organization when people understand that your sole desire is to see them win. John F. Kennedy said, "Victory has a thousand fathers, but defeat is an orphan."[8] Everybody wants to be on the team experiencing victories. As a leader, you create that environment. Every time we gather our entire staff, I do something for them that's over the top. One year, when the Apple Watch came out, we took them to a really nice restaurant and all of them had Apple watches at their table, just because. What do you think that does that do to our

---

7. Quotes from *John Maxwell: Insights on Leadership,* B&H Publishing Group, 2014.
8. Cited in *A Thousand Days,* by Arthur M. Schlesinger Jr., Houghton Mifflin Company, 1965, p. 289.

team morale? There's no end to what people will do for you when they know you truly want them to win.

9. *People desire relationships: provide community.* This is a big deal, now more than ever in our divisive national climate. I like to practice the 101 percent rule: find the one percent you have in common with someone, and give it one hundred percent of your attention. This means thinking, "I don't care who you voted for; but I know we can find some commonality, and once I find it, that's what I'll lean into." God created us for community. What kind of community are you creating in your organization?

10. *People seek models to follow: be an example.* People do what they see. St. Francis of Assisi was speaking with leaders he was preparing to send out. They asked him, "St. Francis, what should we say? How do we take the gospel out into the community?" He replied, "Preach the gospel always, but use words only when necessary." The greatest message you can send to your organization is what you do. If you want integrity in your ministry, begin by being a person of integrity.

CLOSING THOUGHTS

Serving is one of the most powerful tools God has given us. Jesus says that the last shall be first and the first shall be last. In the world system, it's about clamoring to get to the top. In the kingdom, it's about getting to the bottom. The kingdom has an ethic of "the towel". That's the ministry of Jesus Christ. If you embody that servant's heart, you will touch people's hearts and be leading by example. That's what it really all comes down to, in the end.

Pastor Van Moody has a passion for transforming people, organizations, and the world. He has a background in leadership, business and ministry. He writes frequently for The Christian Post and Fox News, and is the author of two bestselling books. Moody lives in Birmingham, Alabama, with his wife and two children, along with their golden-doodle dog, Teddy Bear.

chapter 4

STAYING AHEAD OF THE CURVE

/////////////////

by Pastor Keith Battle

W HEN WE TALK about staying ahead of the curve, we're really talking about the curves in life ahead of us—turns we cannot yet see. Everything I am going to share can be summarized in two words: anticipation and preparation. When it comes to preparing ourselves for the circumstances ahead, we must not be caught off guard. Rather, we must plan and prepare to navigate them in the most Christ-like way possible. I would like to share with you some Biblical ways we can do just that.

PREPARATION IN EACH DECADE OF LIFE

My mentor's name is Bobb Biehl. He's a 75-year-old man who has worked with companies and executives for forty years. Bobb says that every decade of one's life has a theme. For instance, for the first 10 years of a person's life, the theme is *security*: what children need in the first 10 years of their life is somebody to protect them. The second 10 years, the teen years, are all about *self*; lots of teens are self-absorbed during this stage, asking questions of identity and belonging. The third decade can be defined by *survival*: if we do a good enough job as parents, we should allow our children to develop the strength of independence. Then, the next decade is all about *success*—in your thirties, you just want to get to the next thing. In the forties, we shift to a focus on *significance*: we want to do something with lasting value. The fifties is the decade when you hit your *stride*. The *Harvard Business Review* says the best time to hire an executive for any organization is at age 53: by age 53, you've kind of figured life out, and yet you're still young enough to have the energy to lead an organization.

Your sixties is the *strategic* decade. In your sixties, you're smarter than you've ever been. When Forbes Boulevard did research on the wealthiest people in American history, the dominant group said they made their most money in their sixties. That's good news to some of us. That means our best days are still in front of you. Your seventies is the *succession* decade. This is when, if God permits you to live this long, you leave a heritage for your children's children. Your estate planning should already be laid out and finalized, and all the things you built should be in the process of being handed off to others. There's no lasting success without a successor. You have to begin identifying, "Who's going to replace me in doing the things that I've done in my family and profession?"

All of these stages and decades require preparation. There's no way you'll be successful in your sixties if you squander the previous decades, or that your family will be prepared for your passing unless you have taken the steps necessary to build a strategy beforehand. We see an example of preparing for a curve in Scripture: In 2 Chronicles 14, King Asa prepares his army for a time of war during a time of peace. Most of us are caught off-guard during a crisis because we haven't prepared before it hits.

I get a chance to travel and speak at churches in different parts of the country. I can tell which churches value my coming as early as the airport by looking at a few key details: Are the people at the airport when we arrive? Do we have to stand around waiting for them? Let's think about it this way: if Jesus was coming over to your house tomorrow, I guarantee you'd be clearing away the stuff you don't usually clean today. You'd say, "We ain't going to have that on. Put that Bible right there. Move that magazine." So we see that true preparation respects what's coming by being ready for it.

Not only that, but preparation is a revelation: it reveals whether or not I took seriously the opportunity before me. Until the moment of opportunity hits, you don't know whether or not the person is prepared. Take the illustration of a test: a test is the revelation of preparation. You cannot pass a test by accident—you must prepare; it's intentional. It is those who prepare who become successful.

FIVE WORDS TO HELP MANAGE YOUR TURNS

How do we practically put this principle into action in our lives? I'd like to give you five words to keep in mind as we actively prepare to manage our curves before they are upon us.

Research

If you're going to get ahead of the curve, you must be thorough with research. Let's look at a Biblical example of this. In Numbers 13, we see there's a curve coming: the children of Israel, who had been in bondage for years, are on the brink of going into the Promised Land.

> *The Lord now said to Moses, "Send out men to explore the land of Canaan, the land I am giving to the Israelites. Send one leader from each of the twelve ancestral tribes." So Moses did as the Lord commanded him. He sent out twelve men, all*

tribal leaders of Israel, from their camp in the wilderness of Paran. —Numbers 13:1-3 (NLT)

What were these twelve men doing? Research. In the world of business, we call it due diligence. Even though we walk by faith, we must know the facts. What research needs to be done so you are prepared for the opportunities coming around the curve? Some of us are receiving opportunities to cross into spaces we are not prepared for. Each time we move to the next level in life, our elevation is a reminder to be humble—each time we move up, we must learn our new context. Do your research beforehand, and the transition will be feasible.

Here is another demonstration of this principle: in Luke 14, Jesus tells the following parable.

"But don't begin until you count the cost. For who would begin construction of a building without first calculating the cost to see if there is enough money to finish it? Otherwise, you might complete only the foundation before running out of money, and then everyone would laugh at you. They would say, 'There's the person who started that building and couldn't afford to finish it!'

"Or what king would go to war against another king without first sitting down with his counselors to discuss whether his army of 10,000 could defeat the 20,000 soldiers marching against him? And if he can't, he will send a delegation to discuss terms of peace while the enemy is still far away. —Luke 14:28-32 (NLT)

Every elevation has a cost that must be weighed—physically, emotionally, mentally, and spiritually. Can you afford this curve—this elevation? You'd be surprised how many people in ministry suffer stress, anxiety, heart attacks, strokes—health catastrophes—because they fail to accurately count the costs of their lives' demands. What will we do to prepare for our next elevations? This is essential to successfully rounding the curve.

Relationships

Let's return to Numbers 13, wherein the Israelites are about to round their next curve into the Promised Land. Moses sends out the 12 spies, and we see them come back with their report.

But Caleb tried to quiet the people as they stood before Moses. "Let's go at once to take the land," he said. "We can certainly conquer it!"

But the other men who had explored the land with him disagreed. "We can't go up against them! They are stronger than we are!" —Numbers 13:30-31 (NLT)

It is important to be aware of who hinders you and who helps you as you're going into transition. Any time there is a curve in your life, God is going to bring in people to help you transition. Likewise, there will be no opportunity without opposition. The presence of opposition means you are on to something. Moses has people for the move and people against it. It was important for him to listen to those who were aligned with God's will, for Israel's ultimate good, instead of the detractors, if they were going to conquer the land.

Don't waste time and energy fighting those who hinder you: this is what Andy Stanley calls "sideways energy". As you know if you're in leadership of any kind, no leader is omnipotent—we have a limited amount of energy, time, and resources. Wherever I invest my energy, I can't get it back. If I obsess over negative things people say about me, those precious resources will be lost forever. Instead, simply recognize the difference between your assistants and detractors in your transition.

Reverence

If you're in leadership, you must reverence the opportunities over the obstacles. Obstacles are a deterrent for opportunities. The spies' issue was never with the land itself—the opportunity God had promised them—but with the people inside it—the obstacle. Our goal in our faith walk is to see opportunities and remember that they are worth overcoming the obstacles in the way.

We see this play out in the story of David and Goliath. Saul's Israelite army stood 330,000 men strong. Where was their opportunity? Goliath said, "If one of you defeats me, you all have conquered all of us." Saul also had some gifts on the table. Yet, how many of the 330,000 took it? None. The one who did take the opportunity wasn't even in the army.

You're wired in a unique way when you're able to see the opportunity foremost, without ignoring the obstacle. You are then able to help others along, to reassure them that "We're going to be all right." What adds value to an organization is not only someone who can identify problems, but someone who raises solutions to the problems they identify. If you have this insight, you show that you can take a step further than most.

Resistance

Back to Numbers chapter 14: something very interesting happens after this exchange. Moses asks, "Is there food? Are there high walls? What's the fruit like?" What is the purpose of these questions? Moses is performing necessary inquiry into his research.

> *Then the whole community began weeping aloud, and they cried all night. Their voices rose in a great chorus of protest against Moses and Aaron. "If only we had died in Egypt, or even here in the wilderness!" they complained. "Why is the Lord taking us to this country only to have us die in battle? Our wives and our little ones will be carried off as plunder! Wouldn't it be better for us to return to Egypt?" Then they plotted among themselves, "Let's choose a new leader and go back to Egypt!" —Numbers 14:1-4 (NLT)*

What's their motive to go back into the wilderness? We usually attribute negative connotations to the wilderness. For the Israelites, it had been a place of stability and provision—their needs had been met there. While Egypt had been a place of turmoil and bondage, the wilderness offered freedom. They hadn't had to work for food. They'd had manna and quail sent daily to them. They'd had protection from enemies. Now, Moses was saying, "Let's go conquer the land." But the Israelites had gotten so comfortable, they would rather die where they were. It's as if they were protesting, "Don't disturb my comfort, God."

It's astounding how the hardest people to move, many times, are those in comfortable places. To a comfortable person, even a vision connotes discomfort. There is a strong temptation for us to settle in these comfortable spaces and never move forward. The Israelites didn't stop there. They said, "Let's not just stay in the wilderness—let's go back to Egypt." How crazy is that? You know you've lost your mind when you want to go back to Egypt. Whenever you are at the intersection of your next curve, there will be both a pull into your destiny and a pull from your depravity—to go back to what God delivered you from.

In psychology, there's something called "forward recall." Your forward recall causes you to look at a dark situation in your past and only remember the good times; you don't remember what you lost—you just think, "Man, we used to have a good time back then." Forward recall is part of the reason why past times of comfort are so tempting to revisit. They are familiar, while the Promised Land is beautiful, but unknown.

Recognition

In order to stay ahead of the curve, you must recognize that God will do something inside you to communicate that you're curve-ready. The best analogy I can use for this principle is that of a pregnant woman. Not all pregnancies are the same, but one thing many pregnant women experience is morning sickness. A sign that you're *spiritually* pregnant is when you're sick in the morning: sick of going to that job: when you fight to go into work every morning, and every time you wake up, you think, "Oh, God! I've got to go back in there." That's a sign.

Another sign is when you reach a point in "pregnancy"—and I've seen this three times with my wife—where you're just thinking, "I am ready to have this baby any time; just come on, let me get this baby out." Sometimes, in your life, you get that urge, that hunger, and think, "I'm ready to do this."

Another thing that happens when you're pregnant is that start growing—you can't into fit things that you used to fit into. When God matures something in you, you don't fit in the same spaces. That's why maternity clothes are popular. But, unlike pregnant women return to their original sizes, whenever you're pregnant from God, you will never reduce back to the size you once were. These are signs He's taking you into a shift, a curve, in your life.

One last insight in relation to this pregnancy metaphor: prenatal care—and newborn care—is essential. While God may have shown you a vision of your full-grown calling, we invariably give birth to infant versions of these callings. You'll have to develop and nurture that seed until it is full-grown, and this process is by His design. Let's look at a passage in 1 King 19 that showcases the importance of recognizing the curve.

So Elijah went and found Elisha son of Shaphat plowing a field. There were twelve teams of oxen in the field, and Elisha was plowing with the twelfth team. Elijah went over to him and threw his cloak across his shoulders and then walked away. Elisha left the oxen standing there, ran after Elijah, and said to him, "First let me go and kiss my father and mother good-bye, and then I will go with you!" Elijah replied, "Go on back, but think about what I have done to you." —1 Kings 19:19-20 (NLT)

Elisha is about to experience a curve. He has never met Elijah before when he walks up. The Bible says Elisha was taking care of twelve rows of oxen—so we see that he's a farmer. Elijah throws his cloak over him, which was an indication in those times that he was transferring his mantle onto him: Elisha would be Elijah's successor.

Now, remember, Elisha wasn't even in seminary at this time. He's a farmer. This shows that God can give you a curve that doesn't match what you've been involved in up to that point; He can turn you out of your career path into something new. When Jesus began calling people into ministry, He called fishermen and tax collectors. This is a farmer about to be the prophet of Israel. So Elisha says, "Okay, let me say goodbye to my family." Always consult with your family before you go into a turn, because it's going to cost them as well.

Then, the Bible says, Elisha left twelve yoke of oxen standing there. Not only did he leave the oxen, but he slaughtered them and used the plow wood to cook the meat. He gave the meat to the townspeople, which communicated, "Not only am I leaving this, but I am making it difficult to ever go back to it." Whenever you're coming upon a curve, you're going to have to leave something. Most people never move on because they're not willing to let go of what they're holding. We sometimes leave the door cracked on our way out. We might say things like, "We're breaking up, but I am going to keep your number, just in case I made a mistake." There are times when you've got to close off that access so that you don't go back. Elisha severed all ties with his former path.

Research, Relationships, Reverence, Resistance, and Recognition. These five words will immensely help you as you prepare to take the next curve in your life with God. I want to leave you with a few more principles on collaborating with those in your organization during transitions. People are invaluable in this process, and working well with them can make or break your experience in that curve. Here are a few principles to keep in mind.

PREPARING FOR TURNS WITH MULTIPLE GENERATIONS

Something I consider essential in preparation is having relationships with younger people at the table of decision, so that their insight and awareness of cultural shifts keeps us alert. We tend to dismiss other generations because they are unique from ours; but I believe we must be pliable to the wisdom they provide. Other generations key us in to what services need to be provided, how society obtains information, and the different ways things are done today. Including multiple generations at the table is a great way to understand what they need—what our culture needs. How can you best provide your services? You cannot grow as an organization if you ignore future generations.

One way we see this playing out is in the realm of technology in the church. As pastors, we must become comfortable utilizing technology—shepherding those people we can't see. When people have an option as to whether they will get their kids ready and come to church or watch church in their pajamas, many times they will choose to watch from home. Instead of punishing them for this, we must embrace it, because it's going to be the way many do church in the next five to ten years.

You can garner a wealth of creative ideas from young people, and you don't lose your organization's value by doing so; you don't lose who you are at your core—instead, you are able to initiate beneficial changes by listening to others.

HOW TO HELP THOSE WHO ARE AVERSE TO CHANGE

Here are two strategies I recommend for introducing change to those people who may be reluctant or unwilling to accept it.

At some level, we are all averse to change, because it introduces a perceived pain or loss: "This is going to make me uncomfortable or take something from me." If I am trying to encourage a person thinking like this, I have to minimize the risk they perceive. In these conversations, I always reemphasize how important the person's role is—how we need him or her now more than ever. I explain that this change is not for the purpose of making this individual obsolete, but rather to empower the organization to serve more people. I tell this person that they are of intrinsic value to the transition.

The second part of this strategy is encouraging them to see the bigger picture. Helping people see beyond themselves is essential. Reinforce that your purpose is not ultimately about your team. How will this transition impact the world's needs? Share your own personal sacrifices—what you're giving up and wrestling with in the change. Then, show your team how you came to a place where you are on board with it. They'll see that you're invested, as well, and that this goes beyond any one person to the goal of benefiting the world at large.

What decade of life are you in currently? Do you see the word used above as a factor in this time of your life? How are you preparing, through research, relationships, reverence, resistance, and recognition, to tackle the upcoming curve in your life? Who is around you to assist you in walking with God through that transition? My prayer is that you find the strength and wisdom to navigate your turns with grace and peace, in His timing and His way.

Pastor Keith Battle is the founder of Zion Church in Largo, Maryland, a movement helping people become committed followers of Christ by meeting God, growing closer to Him, and serving Him across various locations and technologies. Pastor Keith is married to his best friend, Vicki, and has three children—Asha, Asa, and Kendall.

chapter 5

PRINCIPLES OF ACCOUNTABILITY

///////////////

by Pastor Ralph Martino

I HAVE THE INCREDIBLE opportunity and responsibility of sharing with you a subject that has been life-changing for me. If you understand and apply the principle of accountability, it will change your life, as well. Since the beginning, God has been heavy on accountability. In Genesis 3 we see that, as soon as mankind fails, He asks them, "Where are you? What are you doing?"

God called to the Man: "Where are you?"

He said, "I heard you in the garden and I was afraid because I was naked. And I hid."

God said, "Who told you you were naked? Did you eat from that tree I told you not to eat from?"

The Man said, "The Woman you gave me as a companion, she gave me fruit from the tree, and, yes, I ate it."

God said to the Woman, "What is this that you've done?"
—Genesis 3:9-12 (MSG)

When we hear the "where" and "what" of God, it communicates He is big on accountability. Just as it is important to the God the Father, so it is to Jesus. Jesus chose His business partners carefully. Even Judas, who was close to him, was required to be accountable for himself. We see throughout Scripture that accountability is a key component of God's relationship with humanity.

I am blessed to play sports. When you're on a sports team, you want to be with people who want to win. So, you hold each other accountable—you work out together. However, a lot of people don't want to work out—they want the benefits of what the team has, without being accountable for taking the steps to get there. As a leader, we have to deal with people like this being part of our teams. As an athlete, we see that the Lord graces us over time, giving us the ability to learn the essential nature accountability. When nobody else is working out, guess what? We learn it's time for us to work out. I relearned this lesson again in my experience as an army officer, a college student, and a sole proprietor of an IT consulting firm.

THE PARABLE OF THE TALENTS

What's interesting to note, as a sole proprietor, is that, if you don't market, you didn't eat. I had to set the example by doing things first. In any situation, accountability will quickly ferret out who's real and who's fake. We see this in a Scriptural account relayed by Jesus Christ Himself. Let's take a look at this together. In Matthew 25, the Lord teaches about three different types of individuals. Two of them had similar characteristics, whereas the other one differed.

"It's also like a man going off on an extended trip. He called his servants together and delegated responsibilities. To one he gave five thousand dollars, to another two thousand, to a third one thousand, depending on their abilities. Then he

left. Right off, the first servant went to work and doubled his master's investment. The second did the same. But the man with the single thousand dug a hole and carefully buried his master's money. —Matthew 25:14-18 (MSG)

As a leader, we must pay close attention to what is being communicated. Whether you're sacred or secular, whether you own your own business or not, whether you're a part of ministry or not, this story is significant in discerning who the people in your midst are. The question you ask becomes, "Who in my circle can I delegate responsibility to—who, when I turn my back on them, will keep this moving?"

In the parable, the man is going off on an extended trip, so he calls together his board and begins to explain to them, "I am going off for a while. There's some business opportunities outside of the area. I am going to delegate responsibility." With the delegation of responsibility comes another ability—accountability. The master delegates how? *"depending on their abilities."* IN other words, what he knows about his workers based on how he's seen them in action. What were they able to do with what he gave them? No matter their skill set or resume, everybody still has to go through the necessary testing to ensure they're who they say they are in terms of character.

What did these servants in the parable do? The first man *"went to work and doubled his master's investment."* – I love this – *"The second did the same."* They didn't stay home; they kept the master's wealth growing. They were proactive in the process of reinvestment.

The Lord blessed us to start our IT consultancy firm, Creative Technical Solutions. My aunt loaned me $5,000 to get started. We made sure government contractors and commercial organizations had the personnel they needed. We paid my aunt back, and from that point on we kept growing. Throughout this process, God was sharing with me this truth: You can generate wealth, but the question is what will you do with it once you get it? Is it about the houses? The car? Or is it about reinvesting in what God has called you to do? The Lord taught me how to reinvest, and keep generating wealth, so that we ended up with a massive amount of capital.

Let's move on to the third servant. *"But the man with the single thousand dug a hole and carefully buried his master's money."* This man represents those leaders who keep things static and refuse to invest—to grow. They spend time carefully burying their potential wealth instead of carefully investing. They won't study cryptocurrency, so they don't know what it is or how to use it. They won't study the stock market, because their money is under their mattress in hopes that it will be safe there. In this parable, the master helps us begin to understand the two types of people that we will always encounter: those who are accountable and those who refuse to be held accountable. That's what this parable is all about.

WHAT IS ACCOUNTABILITY?

Accountable people come in stages: you can give one, two, or five talents to them, but we are reassured they will get the job done. Again, whether you're scared or you're secular, you must know those who work around you. If they're going to stay in your circle, they must bring something to the table. Why do you think the master gave them their talents based upon their ability, after all? It's because he knew their character before He handed out their assignments.

People are driven by principles. What is a principle? It's a compelling truth or standard that has been proven, and can be used across any application or platform, without being polluted or diluted. It may be snowing outside, but my principle says I am still going to work. You can hate me, but my principle says I am still going to love you. We must not be emotionally driven, but driven by principles—a greater standard. Because I am principle-driven, you can't pollute my principle. You can't take away from what I know works.

Jesus Christ was also driven. He said, "I *must* be about my Father's work." You must make your principle personal. The most successful people in your circle are those who are accountable. Show me an accountable person; I'll show you a faithful person.

So, moving on to accountability—what is it? Accountability is a willingness and a readiness to do three things:

1. Give account for oneself: our activities and non-activities.

We answer not just for what we do, but what we didn't do. The Bible says,

> *For all the promises of God in him are yea, and in him Amen, unto the glory of God by us. —2 Corinthians 1:20 (KJV)*

In other words, get it done to the glory of God. If somebody asks you to do something, it's either yes or no; accountable individuals understand the importance of yes or no. Do you know what happens when somebody says no? All that means is, I hear in my spirit, "Recalculating." You've got to get it done, regardless of anyone else—no matter what. Then, we give an account of ourselves, firstly to God. We see in Romans 14:12 that,

> *Every one of us shall give account of himself to God.*

Are you willing and ready? As a leader, you must ask the other person this question before you assign them. What have they done to prepare themselves?

2. Accept responsibility for what we have done or not done.

This is the other side of the coin. The days of making excuses are over. If you want more than you have, it requires that you and I understand accountability. Accountability gives birth to responsibility, and responsibility determines whether or not I am being accountable with what God has given me to do. There's nothing worse as a leader than finding suddenly that somebody didn't do what they were supposed to do. We have to accept responsibility for what we've done and what we've not done.

3. *Be willing to disclose our results in a transparent manner.*

Honesty is essential. If someone says to me, "I learned something about myself, sir. I really don't have the skill set to do this, and I was ashamed to tell you that because I know you believed in me," I wouldn't hold that against them. That would mean we could send him to training, and I would cherish his honesty.

Accountability and responsibility require honesty and transparency. If you can't do it, say you can't do it; but keep recalculating. As a leader, when something drops, we pick it up and keep running. That's what we're supposed to do. That's why God gives you the gift of leadership.

What makes a person accountable? What made the servants who received the five and the two different from the servant that only received one talent? Accountability.

THE ACCOUNTABILITY ACROSTIC

I'd like to share with you an acrostic that illustrates accountability, based on the parable of the talents. Each of these elements is a facet of the principle of accountability. Let's go through each of them together.

A—Attitude

The Bible says that the servants "went," "traded," and "made". What would cause somebody to go to work like that? The right *attitude*. They appreciate the fact that God has given them something, that is different from what He's given everybody else. When an individual operates with an attitude of gratitude, it sets them apart. They're thankful for the opportunity to go forth, and they demonstrate it through their attitude. I'm sure you know that there's nothing worse than hanging around folks who have the wrong attitude. This is a crucial starting point.

C—*Character*

What does the fruit on your tree look like? Do you know that having fruit on your tree requires consistency? Jesus said, "Well done my good and faithful servant." He said this to the servants because He had watched to see whether they would be accountable—demonstrate good character—and they had. In contrast, we see that he calls the unfaithful servant, the one with poor character, that he is "wicked" and "slothful." Let that not be any of us.

C—*Conduct*

My character is revealed through my conduct. When the servant who received five went, traded and made, he was excited about what he was doing. His character was revealed through his conduct. Whenever you're on assignment, the enemy is going to try to come up against you. He knows that, if he can stop you from going, we will never make anything. Accountability through conduct says, "I went; I traded; I made. I did what you asked me to do."

O—*Obedience*

When we have the right attitude, character, and conduct come together, it results in obedience. An accountable person obeys at a higher level. The purpose behind this ministry is to raise everybody up to a higher level with God; but guess what? You've got to be willing to obey—believe God for what He has told you. We've got to partner with Him.

U—*United*

Leaders, this is so very important. This letter refers to being united to the vision God has given you. Anybody who comes in to your assignment and tries to create a vision that was not sent from God, who can't bring anything to the table, is divisive. I am principle-driven. I won't get caught up in that kind of maneuvering. I am driven by a greater power. When you hire somebody, ask them, "Here's our vision. Here's where were going. Can you unite with that?" If they can't, it's okay.

Recalculate—next. You won't have to worry if you pray about it: the right people will show up.

N—Network

Individuals bring value to your team through networking. One of the principles that I live by is this: your "network" reveals your net worth. If people don't bring net worth, then they're probably not networked, but only want to tap into yours. You've got to be very careful who's pulling on your jacket. One of the questions that we ask new team members is, "Why are you here? What do you want to get out of this?"

T—Trustworthy

An individual that's accountable is trustworthy. The Lord knew who was going to perform and who would not, but still entrusted them so they could see for themselves that their failure was not with God but with them.

Our whole objective as leaders must be to help those under us to be successful; the only way to help them is not to lie to them, but to help them to understand their capabilities and where they lack. If we can help somebody experience a small victory, that person will want more. With every small victory will come a larger one, and they'll want to be held accountable. That will be the person who will beat you to work, and show up ready to serve.

A—Affinity

Affinity is loving what you do with a passion. Listen to this verse again from the parable.

> *Then he that had received the five talents went and traded with the same, and made them other five talents. —Matthew 25:16 (KJV)*

This servant wasted no time. If you're procrastinating, you're not accountable. You must have an affinity for what you do; if you're serious about what you're doing, get it done and do it with passion. Stop wasting your time and everybody else's time. God rewards those who diligently seek Him, that put in the work.

B—Balance

So many people are out of balance. You and I are comprised of spirit, soul and body. My spirit must stay in balance with God. My soul must stay in balance in between God and what's going on in my life. You can't just be a good husband and not be a good pastor. You can't just be a good pastor and not be a good husband. There has to be balance. What happens when your tires aren't balanced? It pulls you off the straight path of the road. When you and I are out of balance, our human will gets pulled in either direction and will wear out; and then we wonder why we're in burnout. Because we're not balanced.

I –Integrity

We have this document that we use for our leadership—it's an integrity check. We challenge folks when they sit down: "How were you this past week? What did you do?" People who operate in integrity are blessed. God will always bless someone that operates in integrity, because God is a God of integrity. If He can entrust you with something, it's because of the integrity in which you operate in your life.

Accountable people are always learning. Then, they go out and apply. We want to be hearers and doers of the word, so when we go out there, our work is blessed.

I—Invested

If you get me involved in something, I am invested. I don't have time to waste. Do you know what stress is? Stress is taking on today what was supposed to be done yesterday. Whatever you do, invest in it, spirit, soul and body. Additionally, only take on things that God asked you to do. We often take on things God didn't ask us to take on, and end up frustrated, while He's sitting there saying, "I didn't tell you to do that."

T—Temperate

Temperance is self under Spirit's control. Temperate people are not too high, not too low—they are controlled and therefore accountable. The control of the Spirit of the living God leads me and gives me what I need. I've got to be accountable for maintaining this integrity before God.

Y—Yielded

Accountability yields to the right way. Accountable people yield fruit in their lives, and then in the lives of those they lead. When you yield, God will truly bless your life. Don't strive to be sure about your business. Be sure about your God. If you if you take care of His business, He'll take care of yours. God will take care of your business. When you're accountable to God, God will bless every area of your life. You've got to be willing to yield.

If we are stubborn or rebellious, God can't do anything with us. Within the word "accountability" are all of these component parts He is looking for in you. When He sees them, He will pour into your life the power of His Holy Spirit, so you begin to operate and function. Your attitude changes. Your character changes. Your conduct changes. Your obedience heightens. You're unified in the entire process. You're networked like that, and I see that you're trustworthy, and now you have an affinity for everything you're doing. You're balanced in your life, operating in integrity. You're a learner and you're invested, and because you're temperate, you can yield. Glory to God!

HOW TO INSTITUTE ACCOUNTABILITY AS A LEADER

Accountability must be frontloaded. Make sure everybody is aware up front about what is expected of them. If you want me to work, give me a job description and my responsibilities, and then, based upon those, hold me accountable. When frontloaded like this, accountability produces three key things:

1. Healthier Relationships

Wondering why people are always after your job? They assume it's easier than theirs; but they don't realize that the reason it looks easier is because you're accountable. You know the importance of going in and knocking out the work so you don't have to deal with that mess tomorrow.

2. No Last-second Surprises.

When people know what's expected of them, there's no surprises that materialize suddenly. This may sound a bit strict. I've been in the military all my life. I am also a soldier for Jesus Christ. Expectations are essential to both. Eliminate the last-second surprises by instating accountability.

3. Significantly Improved Results

We must be result-oriented. In Mark 11:22-23, the Master says this:

> And Jesus answering saith unto them, Have faith in God.

> For verily I say unto you, That whosoever shall say unto this mountain, Be thou removed, and be thou cast into the sea; and shall not doubt in his heart, but shall believe that those things which he saith shall come to pass; he shall have whatsoever he saith.

Notice what Jesus doesn't say. He didn't talk about the mountain. He didn't talk about the problems. He says, "Speak to it." The God that showed me He had power over the paw of the lion is the same God who will deliver me from Goliath. We must speak to our mountain in the name of Jesus and watch God bring it under subjection. Accountability makes this possible.

Accountability begins with your relationship with your God first. The Holy Spirit is the one in the driver's seat. Get into the passenger seat and begin to listen to Him; He will hold you accountable. When God tells you to move, move. When God tells you to stay, stay. Test every spirit to make sure it is of God.

Let Him lead you to someone who will hold you accountable. That's why Jesus sent them out two by two.

Ultimately, I have an audience of one. My promotion is going to come from God, or it's not coming. Others are not my source. Once He delivers me from that way of thinking, I can live according to Colossians 3:23:

And whatsoever ye do, do it heartily, as to the Lord, and not unto men.

As a closing exercise, write down your one action item after what you have read. What's the one thing you're going to do next in order to be more accountable?

Pastor Ralph Martino is the pastor of First Church of Christ (Holiness) in Washington, D.C. He is the co-founder of Watch and Pray Ministries, whose vision is to reach at risk youth and adults with a non-compromising, Christ-centered end time message. Pastor Ralph is also a spiritual life and leadership coach who counsels, mentors, and helps athletes, executives, and artists achieve their dreams through Biblically-balanced life strategies. He is an author, teacher, entrepreneur, and evangelist.

chapter 6

MAINTAINING YOUR FAITH IN THE PUBLIC SECTOR

///////////////

by Pastor Cornell Brooks

THIS IS AN ANGUISHING hour in our democracy. It is an hour in which our leaders are being tried and tested—held up as public spectacle, held accountable for deeds done in private and in public. It is a moment in which leadership itself is being called into question. Longstanding, ongoing cynicism about the church and other institutions is growing worse. This is a moment in which our privately-nurtured faith is being called publicly into question.

The conversation about maintaining our faith in the public sector could not be more relevant, urgent, or morally necessary than at this very hour. This church, community, and nation has come through a presidential campaign in which we have seen racism normalized, anti-Semitism de-exceptionalized, islamophobia made the norm, and misogyny being screamed. We have seen leaders duck the issues, the questions, and morality. It is right for us to talk about maintaining our faith in the public sphere.

You need not be President of the United States, a member of the United States Senate or House of Representatives, or on the pages of *The New York Times* or *The Wall Street Journal* to be concerned about how we are to maintain our integrity—a compass pointing towards God—in this time. There have been many days where I have been tested, when my faith has been called into question, in which I've anguished over the question, "How do we maintain consistency between what we're called to do and what we, in fact, do?"

This is a matter of central importance and moral urgency for the church; for business leaders; for pastors; for community; leaders; and for folks who just want to walk their talk. How do we maintain our faith in the public sphere? I'd like to study a Biblical leader who did just that, and draw principles from his walk with God that are applicable to our walks today.

MOSES AND PRINCIPLES OF LEADERSHIP

In the book of Exodus, we find a paradigmatic, powerful, and poignant leader in the person of Moses. Moses is described as a transformational leader—someone whose leadership style inspires and catalyzes people onto a trajectory of progress, closer to God. As an emerging leader, Moses has an identity crisis. This is the first principle of leadership I want to share with you.

Moses is raised in the household of Pharaoh, as a kind of semi-Egyptian prince. He has the privileges of Egyptian royalty, but was by birth part of the enslaved Hebrew nation. One day, he looks out on his people and notices the degree to which they were suffering and toiling in their hard labor. He sees an Egyptian oppressing a Hebrew slave, intervenes, and kills the Egyptian. We see here that Moses, as an ascendant leader (though not an aspiring leader), has an identity crisis, for the reason that his identity is shifting based upon his perceptions of justice and injustice. Some of us, as leaders, identify the most with our titles—our status—our accolades—our prominence. We identify with anything and everything except what God has called us to be and do. Our identity should be firmly rooted in who God is, and who we are in Him. In order to reach this point, many of us go through an identity crisis, like Moses did. God has to strip away those things in our lives that we place our identity into before He can take His rightful place.

Later in Exodus, Moses is called to be a leader by God at the burning bush. This is the second principle I want to share with you. God calls Moses to lead the Israelite people out of Egypt. Moses argues with God, pleading for anybody but him to be the designated leader. Many times, we read this passage solely in a negative light—why, after all, would Moses argue with the living God? I'm going to suggest something counterintuitive: People who have an appreciation of the magnitude of leadership aren't always in a rush to be leader. Folks who are hungry for position will always rush to get to the front of the line—many other men would have been all too eager to accept the mantle from God. However, when we appreciate the magnitude of what it is to be called to serve by God, we develop humility. We develop an appreciation for the reality that we cannot lead by ourselves. From Moses, we see the principle that true leaders need never rush to adopt a title, a position, or prestige without God. His timing is perfect, and His ways are higher than ours. When the time does come, be willing to step into it as He leads you.

Moses, this reluctant leader, is known throughout several religious traditions. He is known in Islam—the Quran mentions Moses by name over 130 times more than Muhammad; in Judaism—the first five books of the Torah are called the books of Moses; and in Christianity—Moses stands as a such a liberating figure. In more recent times, African Americans particularly understand Moses's legacy, because we refer to Harriet Tubman as the Moses of her people.

The third principle from Moses's story I want to share is the essential nature of maintaining proximity to God in all you do as a leader. Moses met with God frequently throughout his journey from Egypt to the Promised Land. Interestingly enough, Moses is known as the only person in Scripture invited to meet with God in His presence. It's important for us, as leaders, to understand that our effectiveness has everything to do with divine proximity. You've got to get close to God. Like Moses, stay close to Him, and ask Him what to say and do. Ask God how to act. Ask God how to pray. Ask God how to lead.

LEADERSHIP PRINCIPLES IN ACTION

About four years ago, a civil rights lawyer in New Jersey was working in a small civil rights firm called the New Jersey Institute for Social Justice. This lawyer enjoyed success, passing statewide laws to make life better among those formally incarcerated. If you commit a crime, in many places in this country, it represents a death sentence in terms of employment. So this lawyer had been working for seven years in New Jersey with folks formerly in the Bloods, Crips, Latin Kings, and so on, trying to help these people get jobs. He was quite happy in New Jersey. Then, the lawyer and preacher got a call about serving as the president and CEO of the NAACP. He experienced a bit of an identity crisis: after all, he knew, the NAACP is a big organization. The pool of candidates eventually got narrowed to 30 semifinalists. This lawyer, by the Lord's help, comes out as the chosen candidate: eighteenth president and CEO of the NAACP. I was that man.

Picture being in my shoes: You come into the job of CEO, and you sit down with your team that first year. They tell you that the organization has, currently, a $3 million deficit. There's also a layoff right before you arrive. The second week on the job, a man by the name of Eric Garner in Staten Island loses his life. A few weeks later, Ferguson; Philando Castile; Tamir Rice; Sandra Bland; Laquan McDonald; and Flint. Then comes the Trump nominations; the unrelenting stream of police misconduct; oppression from one end of the country to the other. Now, if you're confident in your abilities, in what you bring to the table in your résumé and profile, that might be sufficient to keep all this from rattling you. However, in my case, because I understood the magnitude of the job and the responsibility, these challenges precipitated a bit of an identity crisis. I had to refocus, to keep in proximity to God, to keep Him as the source of my identity.

As a leader, it's not so much about what you do, but what God does. I came to NAACP anxious about the moment in which we found ourselves, concerned about the $3 million deficit, all the voter suppression in the country, and the other issues. Through the Lord blessing our litigation, we won 11 victories against voter suppression in 12 months. We saw the growth rate go up by 90 percent—young people joining the NAACP high school chapters, college chapters, and youth councils. We saw people wanting to do the work when they saw God's people trying to be good leaders.

I recently got a call asking me to go down to Charleston, SC, to talk about not non-students of Scripture who had been slain in the church by Dylann Roof, in the middle of a Bible study. In that moment, I had to ask myself, "What do I say? What do I do? How do I lead?"

Consulting Moses as the leadership model, I prepared myself and flew to Charleston. Upon my arrival, I got another call from CNN and Wolf Blitzer. He said, "There will be this several million people listening to you as you speak live." I thought, "We don't have a manuscript. There's no pulpit on the sidewalk where I'm going to speak. What do I do?"

There was no time to come up with a plan. Faith requires that we internalize and insulate ourselves with the truth. What you've studied has to be on the inside, in moments like this. You can't wait until a crisis to figure out what kind of leader you're going to be. Without any notes, or any time to prepare, I prayed over my mouth and the Lord led me to say the following. Dylann Roof wore the flag of the nation of Rhodesia when it was under apartheid. He embellished his clothing with the Confederate flag—that insignia of hate. The Lord led me to say that, if Dylann Roof wore a Confederate flag as an emblem of hate as he walked into a church and killed nine people, it's time for that flag to be removed.

I didn't think anything about what I had said, until Congresswoman Maxine Waters said to me, "Do you realize that what people have been whispering about on Twitter and on Facebook is usually put on CNN?" Governor Nikki Haley and the state legislature started debating what God had put into my mouth. I was the most surprised one when the *Today* show and other programs made the video go viral. What I said parenthetically—accidentally—came across as intentional, simply because I listened to the little whisper in my ear.

We need proximity to God in our leadership. We need to be in communication with God, asking, "God, how do I do this? How do I preach this morning? How do I baptize this morning? I know the degree to which I fall short. Between you and me, I've got to be honest with you, God—how can I do what you called me to do, given who I am?" God will then say, "This is who *I* am." Moses went so far as to ask God God's name. Some of us who have been in the church for a long time would do well to ask God, "What's your name? Talk to me. Show me who you are. Reveal yourself to me." Power comes from being close to God knowing who He is, discovering who He is.

After Philando Castile was killed in Minneapolis; and Alton Sterling in Louisiana; and five police officers in Dallas, President Barack Obama called a meeting of the nation's civil rights leaders at the White House.

When you meet with the president, in my limited experience, you meet a half-hour, maybe 45 minutes. There's an aide who begins the meeting, and then the President comes in at the end, shakes hands and asks you how you've been doing. He says a few words and leaves, in the same elegant way he came. In this particular meeting, the President met not for an hour, not for three hours, but for five-and-a-half hours, because he was concerned that Dallas could maybe just go up in flames. He was concerned about what was going to happen.

Here's what I noticed: in moments of crisis, you get a chance to see through a window into the soul of a leader. In moments like that, you can determine whether or not a person is concerned about kingdom priorities or vanity. Are you, as a leader, talking about what makes a difference in people's lives? Are you talking about God's people? Leadership has everything to do with your concern for God's people. The first glimpse we see into Moses's "window" is him risking his life to protect the Hebrew slave. Then, he risks his freedom to protect Israelites. We have to be for God's people, focused on them—focused on the things that matter. The question then arises, how are we to do this—to maintain our faith and demonstrate it through our leadership—in our current, fragmented culture?

UNITY IN A POLARIZED CULTURE

In a time where people are polarized racially and politically, how do we lead in unity?

In my experience, I have found that some people, in a church or an organization, come into a community with certain ethnic and racial assumptions about how it will look. They think something like, "This is my church—my organization—and it represents people who look like me." The important truth to remember is that, even at the family level, the faces of any community will be constantly shifting. Things change. In every culture, we see diversity.

In order to lead well, especially in this nation, we must practice inclusion in our communication, in our worship style, and in the way in which we do ministry. It is our responsibility as leaders to make sure everybody feels like they are part of the work. Underscore inclusion in every aspect if your leadership—in everything you focus on. If your church or organization is going to grow in multicultural, multiracial, multiethnic, and multigenerational America, you've got to diversify your outreach. Once you get the diversity of people in your community, it's going to be reflected in the work that you do.

How should churches speak into the political and justice issues of the day? Many religious leaders are outsourcing justice in the present time. They think, "Let young people handle issues of justice. Let the civil rights groups handle those topics. They are too controversial, and they get in the way of ministry." In addition, there is a fear among many pastors, who have been falsely taught, that if they agree to speak about political issues of the day, they will lose their tax exempt status—that their ministries will be in peril. Conversing about the hot-button issues doesn't seem worth that cost.

Let's be clear about the reality. We must stay involved in the crucial issues happening outside the church doors. Your congregation is living in the world every day—these issues affect all of us. If you're not talking about what the people in your pews are tweeting about, they aren't going to pay much attention—they won't understand where you're coming from; and we won't understand them. We cannot sit idly by and take no action. We, as God's people, have got to use tools. Moses didn't simply pray on the way out of Egypt, right? He took action. The people marched through the Red Sea—they didn't stand around waiting to see what would happen. Likewise, we have got to take a stand—to speak—to be involved.

There are many differing opinions in any community—the church isn't excluded from this. It's important, within the house of God, to have grace and appreciation for theological differences. Everyone will, at some point wrestle with how to answer God's call in terms of pursuing justice. What gets me concerned is when there's no conversation at all. You and

I may disagree about how to best feed the hungry. There are some folks who believe that the church is literally the best provider in terms of feeding the poor. Others believe it's the government. We may disagree about how it's done, but may the Lord help the church if we at any point stop talking about the need for it to be done.

CLOSING THOUGHTS

Maintaining your faith in the public sector, when it comes down to it, is about being spiritually authentic and consistent. Leadership is not a performance. It's not about how many times you get your name in the paper. It's not about how well and what people think of you. It's about being true to your call, all the way from the starting line of Egypt to the edge of the Promised Land. It means living out your calling until God calls you home. When you hear God calling you, answer Him, be steadfast, and do not grow weary in well doing.

People are looking for leaders who are good examples. They are looking for strong role models. They're looking for people who practice the eloquence of example. Help us, God, like Moses, to tremble in the face of leadership because we appreciate the gravity and the weight of it. Help us to be humble, and not lust after prestige or power or position. Help us to understand that we have to look into your face, seek your face, and seek to hear your voice. Help us to understand that if we're going to lead, if we're going to have faith in our private lives that reflects what needs to happen in public, we've got to count on you. Bless all that we do to draw near you; help us answer the call in the ways you would have us; and, God, if by chance we differ with one another in our opinions of how that should be done, let us differ while drawing close to you, and doing what you would have us to do. Amen.

A fourth-generation ordained minister, civil rights attorney, social justice activist, coalition builder and writer, Cornell Brooks served as the 18th President and CEO of the NAACP. While there, he led the organization in securing 11 victories against voter suppression in 12 months. Brooks is Professor of the Practice of Public Leadership and Social Justice at the Harvard Kennedy School. He is also Director of The William Monroe Trotter Collaborative for Social Justice at the School's Center for Public Leadership, and a visiting scholar at Harvard Divinity School.

chapter 7

SAYING YES TO GOD WITHIN YOUR SPHERE

////////////////

by Bishop Harry Jackson

COULD IT BE THAT, at this moment, God is stirring the pot in America—challenging us to deal with major social ills in our culture? The book of Hebrews tells us that the word of God will shake everything that can be shaken, and only things of the kingdom will remain.

> *He has promised, saying, "Yet once more I shake not only the earth, but also heaven." Now this, "Yet once more," indicates the removal of those things that are being shaken, as of things that are made, that the things which cannot be shaken may remain. —Hebrews 12:26-27 (NKJV)*

I believe we're in this moment. As an example, think about the NFL controversy, and what has gone on in that situation. I believe we see God revealing the hearts of individuals for the higher purpose of exposing the sin we've been dealing with for 400 years. No matter what side of the race question you're on, we are beginning to see that all of America has a problem with race. God is stirring the pot—shaking the earth—to reveal this, as well as many other social ills.

The problems go far beyond racism. Consider personal and corporate greed. It may be that America's original sin was a combination of racism and greed. Slave trade was founded around the motivation of making money.

Consider today's rampant sexism. Surely, you've heard of countless cases of men in the news, exposed, sexually harassing people.

The world knows how to sin on an expert level.

The application of this knowledge looks different, depending on what sphere of influence you occupy. If you're a business owner, you're faced with a choice: are you going to address the race problem—the sexism problem—the greed problem—in your environment? Are you going to help people come into their own personal destinies? Church leaders, respectively, must minister in a way that encourages people to take risks to address these ills. We need people involved in the political system to address some of these issues. Some problems, in contrast, are heart problems, and require a heart transformation.

There's only one group with the ability, the anointing, and the authority to make a difference in the life of the nation—to heal the racial divide, the class divide, AND the sex divide. It's the church of the living God. We have to take ownership of the fact that God is stirring the pot, revealing divisions. The only unifying factor in this season are Christians empowered by the church.

THE SEVEN MOUNTAINS

So how do we make changes? I'd like to talk about six or seven "gap areas" where God's moral law and our culture say different things. Then, we'll examine how God directs us, as the Church, to begin to heal these gaps.

Prophetic voices can create guidance and protection for the nation. When revelation and illumination comes from

God, they provides steps of action, guidance, and protection. We see this exemplified in the prophet Ezekiel, in the Old Testament.

And the word of the Lord came unto me, saying,

Son of man, prophesy against the prophets of Israel that prophesy, and say thou unto them that prophesy out of their own hearts, Hear ye the word of the Lord;

Thus saith the Lord God; Woe unto the foolish prophets, that follow their own spirit, and have seen nothing!

O Israel, thy prophets are like the foxes in the deserts.

Ye have not gone up into the gaps, neither made up the hedge for the house of Israel to stand in the battle in the day of the Lord. —Ezekiel 13:1-5 (KJV)

While it's true that not every Christian is in the prophetic office, it is true that, in the kingdom of God, everybody should at some level be hearing from God and speaking for God—an ambassador for the Lord. Where there's moral breakdown, we come and declare God's will in the gap. We must overcome by revelation, proclamation and demonstration, like Ezekiel did.

Ezekiel is in captivity under the judgement of God in Babylon when his work starts out. God is saying here to His people, "If you would've gone into the gap and declared my word, I, God, would've backed you up." Essentially, Ezekiel's message is that God is judging the Israelites because they did not have the temerity or wisdom to confront social problems and call the people into conformity to the God's Word. Therefore, God had to come down on them as a people. All God has to do in order to show them the error of their ways is simply back off. He lets them go their own way, and without his guidance, they're would be in trouble. Without His guidance, you and I are in trouble, as well.

I want to introduce a concept that illustrates our spheres of influence in today's world. The idea is called "The Seven

Mountains of Societal Influence, and was constructed by Bill Bright, who founded Campus Crusade for Christ. Each mountain represents a sphere of influence in which that gap exists, between God's will and our culture's messages. As believers, our calling is to occupy and scale and have dominion over these mountains, by exercising our gifts and callings in the spheres God has called us to occupy. Let's take a look at each of the mountains. Try to pinpoint which mountain(s) God has placed you in, or called you to move into, as we go.

1. Religion/The Church

The church, or religious, mountain is a mountain of influence in every culture. In America, we see it heavily centered on Christianity; but in other nations, the religious mountain is occupied by Islam or some other belief system. These are places worldwide where heavy influence lies. Has God called you to serve in any capacity in the religious sphere?

2. Family

Family is perhaps the most foundational aspect of any society. In families, children are raised in a certain set of beliefs; parents wield immense power to shape the lives of the next generations. Families also hold the potential to wreak destruction and damage on the lives of its members. If God has called you, in any capacity, to uphold the Biblical integrity of your family, it is no small task.

3. Education

The educational mountain is no small one, either. My daughter, who loves Bishop Grier, is a Williams College Little Ivies school undergrad; she's actually done a couple of master's degrees at Harvard, as well. I hear from her about the planting of seeds that are anti-kingdom in the educational realm. Sometimes the academy has a way of painting pictures that subtly undermine foundational things we as Christians believe in. If that mountain is left unpenetrated with gospel thinking and gospel leaders, it will become a force that works against the gospel.

4. Government

The government mountain is a realm of influence and authority in which you can see kingdom opportunities. Unfortunately, many Christians have an aversion going into the government mountain. We need leaders and thinkers in this realm, perhaps now more than we ever have. It is not a mountain to be spurned, but a field ripe for harvest.

5. Media

Reporting truthfully, objectively, and in a God-honoring way is a skill that has become rare in our culture today. Debates on news channels have become full of searing words and personal attacks. The facts have become lost in translation. Opinion pieces have outnumbered objective reporting. While Christians have some outlets in this mountain, the potential for reform and redemption of the media industry has, in many ways, only begun. How will the church exemplify the fruits of the Spirit in how we report the events of the world? How will we be examples to our coworkers and constituents in media?

6. Arts and Entertainment

Arts and entertainment is another mountain ripe for influence. When you start creating movies; when you are involved in communications outside of the church; when you write books or paint paintings or recite poems or put on plays; we all know these things have a major cultural impact. If God has creatively gifted you, don't see your calling as a lesser or superfluous one. Every night, people take in shows, songs, and messages through the arts. You have the power to change someone's life.

7. Business

The economic, or business, mountain is another area of influence. Major corporations, how they operate, what they do, how they employ their money, is critical—especially as we consider those issues of race, sexism, and greed. Christian businesses have multiplied profoundly in recent years. How will we show Christ in our practices and procedures? How will we start to close the gap—heal the broken business mindset—in our world?

We want to studying the seven mountains so that Christians understand what sphere of influence they're called to, can equip themselves to do excellent work, and so they can use their spiritual authority to impact the mountain, and the world. You and your family are called to influence there's a sphere. God wants to anoint us to take territory. We must pray and fast, yes; but we also need to do business well. We need to make good movies. We've got to operate ethically in our businesses. We've got to reclaim the Godly family. We've got to get to the tops of these mountains, and reclaim the United States of America.

Our ministries on the seven mountains begins with intersession and alignment with God's assignment. Your business, your government position, your ministry, must be aligned. What's your mountain? For the last year, I have had a prophetic assignment to the governmental sphere. It has been costly. It has been challenging. But God wants us to move into His will, no matter the cost.

MOVING INTO HIS WILL

There's a false dichotomy in American thought that says secular and religious life is separate. The Bible says this in the book of Psalms:

The earth is the Lord's, and the fullness thereof; the world, and they that dwell therein. —Psalm 24 (KJV)

There's no room for secular versus sacred. It's all God's territory. If we say secular versus sacred, we abdicate our inner responsibility to take dominion. That false dichotomy keeps us in our religious ghettos.

In 2004, I'd just finished coauthoring a book with George Barna called *High Impact African-American Churches*. It was based on a study of 400 African American churches studied their devotional habits and church policies. It's great to be able to coauthor with someone of that stature for me. That book thrust me into a new realm. In this period of about six weeks, I got seven prophetic words. People were coming who had not conferred with this evidence saying, "You are supposed to prophesy outside the walls of the church." They said to me, "God says, 'You're going to be on Fox, CNN, etc..'" I thought, "I don't want to be on Fox and CNN. I don't know how this is going to go." All in all, seven people prophesied this to me: "In the name God, He told me to tell you..." I realized, even though I was not feeling it at that time, that I may need to pray about it after receiving all this input. So I prayed.

The Lord said to me, "I need you to preach on some of the national issues of your day. I want you to say this, this, and this." He gave me specific direction about telling our church what I was going to do in the upcoming election: that I was going to break out of the mold. I was not going to vote along the same party lines. I was looking to see a difference made, so I made a statement about what I would do as a citizen. I made it clear: "I am not telling you what to do. I am just saying this." I did exactly what I felt the Lord was showing me. The next day, there was a manifest presence of God in the services. Folk began to breakout into tears, weeping over the situation we find ourselves in, especially with regard to the African American plight. My message was that God wanted righteousness and justice to be manifest through the church and our nation, and it resonated with the congregation.

Righteousness is right standing with God: doing things that are aligned with holiness. Justice is something you create for others in the name of the Lord. When righteousness and justice meet, it shows us God is enthroned. God can rule and reign and manifest Himself in a greater way when His people create an atmosphere of righteousness and justice.

And I sought for a man among them, that should make up the hedge, and stand in the gap before me for the land, that

I should not destroy it: but I found none. —Ezekiel 22:30 (KJV)

When they couldn't find a man, Ezekiel said yes to God in his sphere. Will you say yes to God in your sphere?

In America, many of us go into work in our sphere in a survival mode. These individuals are, I'd say, at level one in what they're trying to do. Only when we get past survival mode are we able to realize, "God wants to bless me. It's okay if I make some money. I am the blessed of the Lord." At that point, we can operate in principles that bring increase from Him—we start taking the mountain.

The third level is a little higher than simply getting blessed. The third level of operating in your sphere, I believe, is when you use the spiritual principles you've learned—spiritual weapons, if you will—to influence your mountain. When you take ownership of your place, your sphere of influence, and act in faith, God begins to highlight and use you as a witness.

The fourth level is when you are able to see the opportunity for societal transformation and understand, "Hey, I can change culture by being a model business. I can influence others who follow me, and I can take the business mountain (or the government mountain). I can take my part of it, my sphere of influence." All of these levels lead to one purpose: The Lord wants to exalt the kingdom and His agenda.

But in the last days it shall come to pass, that the mountain of the house of the Lord shall be established in the top of the mountains, and it shall be exalted above the hills; and people shall flow unto it.

And many nations shall come, and say, Come, and let us go up to the mountain of the Lord, and to the house of the God of Jacob; and he will teach us of his ways, and we will walk in his paths: for the law shall go forth of Zion, and the word of the Lord from Jerusalem. — Micah 4:1-2 (KJV)

Mountains are powerful spheres of influence. Hills are intermediate spheres of influence. So this verse sounds kind of poetic. What's Micah talking about? He's talking about grassroots power. In the invisible realms, God's kingdoms rule can supersede and be preeminent over every other sphere of influence.

If you're born again, you can hear from God, speak from God, and, at some level, be an ambassador for God. Amen? Now, that doesn't mean you've got to start eating wild locusts. But I want to examine two things that can cause prophetic voices to "go back." What hinders us, or taints our efforts in, conquering our mountains? Two things.

1. *Bad Motives.* If your core motive is personal gain, power and ambition, you're off to a bad start. You've heard about Balaam, the false prophet in the Old Testament, who wanted money and honor. Many of our ministries are straight, honest, God-promoting, kingdom-oriented endeavors; but some folks are in ministry simply for the money. Examine your deepest motivations for doing what you're doing. Is it approval? Pride? Greed? Vanity? Insecurity?

2. *Unconfessed Sin.* If we harbor anger, bitterness, racism, or pride in our hearts, these pollute our gift so that it's not pure. Consistently allow God to examine your spirit and bring to your attention anything in you that does not glorify or serve His purposes.

THE HEART OF A PROPHET

What we've got to do is develop the heart of a prophet.

Moreover he said unto me, Son of man, eat that thou findest; eat this roll, and go speak unto the house of Israel. —Ezekiel 3:1 (KJV)

At the end of chapter 2, God had told Ezekiel all the sins of his people and the judgments written against them. These are all contained in this scroll. Ezekiel eats the scroll, and it's like honey to his lips. Revelation that comes from God is sweet. Afterwards, Ezekiel has an appetite for spiritual things. God tells him to sit by the river and watch for seven days. What you'll find is that compassion comes from observing people. God is trying to develop compassion in Ezekiel.

Many of us get the revelation that something is wrong, and we're all-consumed by it: we point out what's wrong, but we haven't processed the message enough to move beyond bitterness and anger. We must come to a place where, by His power, we're able to release a healing word, tempered by empathy, to those to whom we minister.

Take the issue of race, for example. a white friend of mine has a desire to educate other whites about their privilege; I am coaching this man in this endeavor. I told him one day, "Bro, you can say a right thing in a wrong way, and make folks say, 'I don't want to hear you.' Or, you can allow God to temper your spirit, and deliver a hard word in a way that people receive it. Then, you'll truly be a prophet, rather than a conspiracy-theory-oriented hater."

So many times, our emphasis is on speaking a thing versus hearing a thing. If I make something up that is not anchored in a revelation from the word, it will have very little balance. We're going into demonic strongholds, and if our swords are made out of plastic, somebody's going to get hurt. I emphasize starting with revelation so God grounds you. Then your platform is anchored on what God told you.

God is going to make you work through personal issues in the arena in which you are to minister, so that you minister out of a pure spirit; so you can be a healing answer in times of troubled waters. Could it be that your heart is the only thing limiting the dimensions of your exposure, the fruitfulness of your life, how much truth you really process, and how much you can represent the king as you declare what He has shown you? We've got a place where we can be effective. God's got a kingdom message He wants to bring forth through what we do, in addition to blessing what we do. We must move with Him, and be His ambassadors.

Bishop Harry Jackson Jr. is the senior pastor of Hope Christian Church in the Washington, D.C. area. He also serves as the Presiding bishop of the International Communion of Evangelical Churches. He founded The Reconciled Church conference and the High Impact Leadership Coalition. He has appeared on many television shows discussing matters of public policy, and has published several books.

chapter 8

LEADING FROM THE MIDDLE

//////////////////

by Pastor Jeff Smith

M Y ASSIGNMENT TODAY is to talk to you about leading from the middle. Whether you're in a ministry, business, or any other organization, this is something we will all deal with at some time. I want to share a bit about my leadership journey, and why the topic of leading from the middle is meaningful to me.

My background is both corporate and ministerial. I went to school and graduated with a finance degree, then went into corporate America, where eventually I started in banking as a management trainee. When I left the bank, I was headed up the corporate trust division, and there was great favor and opportunity given to me. I had the opportunity to be the first African American to have an office in the trust department of a major bank in the northwest Ohio area. As I matriculated through that whole process, leading from the middle was something that became very important to me. I left banking and went into ministry, on staff at Cornerstone Church in

Toledo, OH, where I served for nearly 20 years. My position was as a pastoral assistant, which allowed me to see the ministry from several different vantage points. By the time I left the church there, I was the number two guy there.

As you move through spheres of influence and have different responsibilities, learning the art of leading from the middle is hugely significant. Hopefully we can make a contribution to your understanding of this particular dynamic.

FOUR CHARACTERISTICS OF LEADING FROM THE MIDDLE

When we talk about leading from the middle, there are four concepts you really want to keep in the forefront of your mind. These will give you the ability to capitalize on and realize your potential in your position.

1. Awareness

Awareness is one of the most important things for us to consider. Awareness answers the question "Where do I fit in the organization?" I have to be aware of what my sphere of responsibility is if I am going to navigate my space effectively.

2. Accountability

Accountability deals with the question "What are my deliverables—to the tier ahead of me, those on my same plane, and those beneath me?" I am accountable to make sure I am executing those deliverables on each plane.

3. Collaboration

When you're leading from the middle you have the unique, strategic ability to collaborate, build bridges, and be a conduit of information. This answers the question, "What relationships can I maximize on?"

4. Trust

You must build trust along all levels of the organization. You have to have mutual confidence built with the tier above you, the tier you're on, and the tier below you. Trust answers the question, "How am I building trust all the way around?"

When you practice these four characteristics, you'll be equipped to lead. However, in order to be able to lead from the middle with excellence, we also must examine some of the main challenges that arise for us there.

SEVEN CORE CHALLENGES OF LEADING FROM THE MIDDLE

Sometimes, middle-ground leadership is not as clean as the image we have in our minds. It can feel as if you're being pulled from every angle. There are frustrations. Let's take a second to do an exercise. On a piece of paper, write down the top three challenges you have encountered in leading from the middle. To some extent, everyone is leading from the middle. Whether you're a senior pastor, a business owner, or a minimum-wage employee, there's always potential for leadership.

When I posed this question to the Renaissance Leadership Network gathering in March of 2017, they voiced several challenges of leading from the middle, including the following:

- Personnel
- Resources
- Communication
- Being Intentional
- Respect
- Defining Expectations
- Skills, or Insufficient Training
- Vision Casting
- Lack of trust
- Timeliness
- Morality
- Leadership conflicts

- Prioritization
- Implementing Change
- Empowerment
- Intimidation, or fear

What are your three answers? Keep them nearby. I want to explore seven challenges that address every answer to this question.

1. THE TENSION CHALLENGE

In the middle, you possess a degree of decision-making authority, but you don't have the last say. The tension challenge arises when you make a decision and somebody reverses it; or, when you're hesitant to make a decision because you don't know if you'll receive support.

We must learn how to lead despite the restrictions placed on us. No matter who you are or where you are in an organization, nobody is leading without restrictions. Even the senior leader has to work within restrictions. There are some things inside of your sphere of control. There are other things that aren't; let those things go. The tension challenge rears its head when you try to control what you aren't supposed to control.

Another note along this line: Never violate the trust given you. If we're not careful, we can become impulsive, and make a decision where we're not supposed to make one. As we discussed earlier, trust is formed with those above, alongside, and below you. Never violate any of those trust ties.

2. THE FRUSTRATION CHALLENGE

The frustration challenge originates out of following an ineffective leader. I would venture to say that any leader can point to a time when they were serving under an ineffective leader. There are insecure leaders, micromanaging leaders, selfish leaders... How do we deal with the frustration of serving under them?

First of all, understand that your job is not to fix the leader. I know I just popped somebody's bubble; but this is an impossible aspiration. Your job, rather, is to add value to the leader. If the leader won't change, you've either got to change your attitude or your address. You have a decision to make. Either way, you can't stay in your current position if you're going to become toxic to the leader and the organization.

Two things that you can do to add value to a leader: complement the leader's weakness, and support their strengths. Complementing a leader's weaknesses is accomplished through asking permission. You might notice an area they're not as skilled in a certain area, and say, "Would it be alright if I formulate a plan to help us here?" Then, the leader doesn't feel that it's you versus them, but that you're all in it together. Supporting their strengths is coming alongside admirable areas in their leadership and working together to improve things as a whole.

3. THE MULTI-HAT CHALLENGE

In the middle position, you can wear a lot of different hats. You might step out of a meeting where you've just received a direct report, turn around, and suddenly be in a meeting with your supervisor. We have to learn how to navigate these fluctuations fluently.

Know what hat to put on, and enjoy it. Think to yourself, "What is my role in this room?" When I'm in with the senior pastor, my role is different than when I meet with one of the departments I oversee. As you move forward, you end up wearing fewer hats, but you have to wear them more excellently. You move from being a generalist to a specialist, but you have to be proficient at those few things.

Your communication should always match the hat you're currently wearing. The way you communicate to those above you should have a certain tone, a certain language. When you're communicating to those beneath you, you will employ a different tone. you've got to know what hat you're wearing, and then make sure your communication matches it.

4. THE EGO CHALLENGE

The ego challenge comes into play when you're feeling as if your efforts are hidden from the rest of the world. You may think, "No one is recognizing the stuff I'm doing. I'm being overlooked in the grand scheme of things." Our ego gets challenged in the day-to-day operations of the organization.

Remember that consistently good leadership does not go unnoticed. This is essential. Joseph is a gleaming example of this: as he went through different stages in life, the capacity he had always caused him to rise to the top. Just keep on doing good. In addition, don't develop "destination disease." Sometimes, we get our sights set on the next step and start only dreaming about where we're going. When you start focusing on where you're going instead of where you're at, something is going to get dropped. Focus on your duties, not your dreams. Matthew recounts these words of Jesus:

His lord said to him, 'Well done, good and faithful servant; you have been faithful over a few things, I will make you ruler over many things. Enter into the joy of your lord.' — Matthew 25:23 (NKJV)

If I focus on the much ahead and not the little in my hand, I'll never get to the much. But if I am excellent in little, much is assured. So think about your responsibilities, not your rewards.

We must keep an abundance mentality rather than a scarcity mentality. A scarcity mentality begins to feel claustrophobic: we think, "There's not enough acknowledgment, opportunity, credit, or resources." This thinking sets you on a path to begin competing with those around you. However, when you have an abundance mentality, you realize there is enough. You free yourself from having to compete. That's where we ultimately want to be.

5. THE FULFILLMENT CHALLENGE

The fulfillment challenge happens when you desire to be out in front instead of in the middle. You want to be in the driver's seat—to be the decision-maker—to have the title.

Leadership is more about disposition than position. We have to be careful how we define leadership: it's not a title. It's influence. Develop great relationships—above, across and beneath. Relationships are perhaps one of the most valuable commodities you have as a leader. Help others win. Everybody wants to win in life, and if you figure out how to help people win, you'll always be in demand.

Consider this passage where Jesus calls his disciples from their livelihoods as fishermen:

Then Jesus said to them, "Follow Me, and I will make you become fishers of men."—Mark 1:17 (NKJV)

We tend to read that and just keep going, but let's put ourselves in the disciples' space. Jesus is someone they don't know, who's not even in their field—He's a carpenter. Yet He says to them, "Follow me and I'll make you." What's astounding is that they drop their nets and follow this guy. If somebody showed up at your job tomorrow and said, "Quit your job. Follow me. I'm going to make you," would you do it? Would you trust them? What gave the disciples the confidence to drop what they knew to pursue what they didn't know?

People follow when they see a leader's ability to get them to the next level. Jesus said, "Follow me and I'll make you. I'll bring out of you what you didn't even know you had in you. I'll get you to the next level." When we talk about helping others win, we must develop that capacity. Help others get to the next level. Invest in them, and bring out in them what they didn't even realize in themselves. When you do that, they are sure to follow you.

6. THE VISION CHALLENGE

The vision challenge comes into play when you are called to champion a vision you didn't create. This isn't a simple or easy task.

When you choose to invest in a vision, instead of simply watching from the outside, that makes all the difference—the vision then shifts from *his* vision to *our* vision. One of the things I had to do in my pastoral assistant job was embrace the senior pastor's vision as my own. You have to learn to see yourself as a complement, not a competitor, to those above you.

The Bible says,

Two are better than one,
Because they have a good reward for their labor.
—Ecclesiastes 4:9 (NKJV)

When we understand we're in this thing together, great reward comes into our hands at every level.

7. THE INFLUENCE CHALLENGE

The influence challenge involves leading others beyond your positon. If you limit yourself to thinking about your job as limited to a position, your world will shrink. If you think outside of your title, and invest in others beyond its limitations or requirements, your world will expand.

Why will people follow you? Five main reasons:

Position

Permission developed in relationship. People say, "I want to follow you because of the relationship we have."

What you **Produce**. People want to be part of a team that's accomplishing something big.

People development. People realize they are better with you, and want to be on your team.

Personhood. People respect who you are.

None of these seven challenges are impossible for you to overcome. You *can* be effective at leading from the middle. To finish, we'll look at some ways to directly apply the characteristics and challenges we've covered and put them into practice in your leadership role.

THREE DIMENSIONS OF LEADERSHIP

I want to provide you with some suggested courses of action, in three areas that you lead from when you're in the middle. Let's look at principles on leading up, leading across, and leading down.

Leading Up

These practices are applicable to relationships with supervisors, bosses, executives, and those whom you support.

Lead yourself well. One of the biggest things you can offer is self-management. If I can lead myself exceptionally well, I show I'm a great asset to the one I support.

Lighten your leader's load. Think of ways to take weight off your leader's shoulders. You'll become invaluable, and stay in demand.

Be willing to do what others won't. Don't think unwanted tasks are beneath you. Serving is one of the key ways you'll advance. Jesus said, "I came to serve." The Bible says if we humble ourselves, He will exalt us.

Do more than manage: lead. Management maintains. Leadership moves things forward. Take what your organization has put into your hands and multiply it.

Invest in relational chemistry. This takes time and energy. Ask yourself, "How can I build a better relationship with the one I'm serving?"

Be prepared when you take your leader's time. You want to make sure you are prepared beforehand for every minute you spend with your leader. For every minute, you should take five minutes of preparation. Think of what you want to say and the information you want to exchange. Think of what you need or what your leader needs, and be respectful of his or her time.

Know when to push... and when to back off. There will be times you will need to push an idea or perspective; but there are other times you need to back off. Knowing the difference is critical.

Become a go-to player. Be someone who delivers in the midst of stress, difficulties, crisis, and hard times. You'll be indispensable, and people will go to you in their time of need.

Be better tomorrow than you are today. Always be developing and bettering yourself.

Leading Across

This section deals with relationships with peers—those in the same sphere of leadership as you.

Complete the "Leadership Loop". What is the leadership loop? It goes like this: Caring, learning, appreciating, contributing, verbalizing, leading, and succeeding. The loop is about a person of influence, and making sure your organization is succeeding. It gets completed when you believe and live out the truth that, "We're all in this together."

Be a friend. Understand that you're not competing with one another. You are colleagues, completing one another.

Avoid office politics. Politics has to do with the root of interest. When you get caught up in office politics, the interest is a competing one. Always keep the interest of the organization central.

Expand your circle. Continually build and invest in relationships.

Let the best idea win. Be open enough to embrace whatever the best idea is, rather than thinking you must defend yours or compete against the ideas of others. That's how great ideas get assassinated. You're not responsible to come up with all the answers. You simply have to recognize the best answer and embrace it.

Don't pretend you're perfect. Don't pretend like you don't ever make mistakes. You'll hinder your ability to develop relationships by isolating others.

Leading Down

This section deals with those who report to you or are positioned below you in the organization. Take time to see those reporting to you as individuals.

See everyone as a 10. This is the idea of giving everybody an "A" on their paper from the start. Rather than seeing someone as an "F" student, see them as an "A" student. People will want to live up to that standard.

Develop each team member as a person. Everybody is not trainable in the same manner. You want to look at your team and be able to say, "This is what motivates this one, and this is what inspires this one." Develop them as individual people, not necessarily as a group.

Place people in their strength zones. If you get the right people in the right places, the right things happen. If your team is coming in expecting you to have all the answers, one idea that helps growth is to ask them in return, "What do you think? How would you approach this situation?" This fosters creativity and collaboration, and keeps you from coming on too strong.

Model the behavior you desire. When leading down, be an example of what you want to see presented.

Transfer the vision. Deposit vision in those beneath you. One big way to do this is providing them with the "why" of your endeavors, and not just the "what." Explain to them why this is important, and the impact that will be made as a result of your working together.

Reward Results. Acknowledge, recognize, and share the rewards with others when you have a victory.

There are doubtlessly challenges and frustrations to be considered when you lead from the middle. However, if you remain grateful for your sphere of influence, maximize what you've been given, and do everything unto the glory of God, there is also abundant benefit and potential available to you. What are some ways you can reframe or tackle the three challenge areas you wrote down earlier? Who can you invest in more as you re-evaluate your position? How is God calling you to lead from the middle?

Jeff Smith is Lead Pastor of Strong Tower Ministries in Fredericksburg, Virginia, a vibrant and diverse congregation of nearly 2000. In addition, he serves as Director of Cornerstone Global Network under the leadership of Bishop Michael Pitts, a network of over 60 churches throughout the United States, Mexico, and the U.K. Jeff has been married to his college sweetheart Nicola since July 11, 1992, and they are the proud parents of Lauren, Kristin, and Jeffrey.

chapter 9

MAINTAINING FOCUS DURING TRANSITION

///////////////

by Bishop B. Courtney McBath

WE ARE IN SOME INTERESTING and unique times today; yet I have found that God does His best work in chaos. My prayer is that, as we manage transitions—politically, spiritually, and personally—we keep God first and foremost in our sights. In His Word, God says that if we acknowledge Him in all of our ways, He will direct our paths. I believe this is true, and I want to help us maintain this focus during some of the tumultuous periods of change we face in daily life.

In the midst of our transitions, what becomes critical for us to remember is that God's position never changes. Sometimes, what we need is not necessarily new information—a new revelation or piece of advice—but rather, additional emphasis on the fundamentals we have already hidden in our hearts. Imagine where we would be today if the body of Christ in America became obedient to merely 30 percent of what we've been taught. Can you imagine the revolution this would bring? This wouldn't require a new word from God—simply enacting the truths He's already given us. Most of the time, a simple review and practical application of what we already know is all we need to manage where we are, and what we face.

DANIEL AS AN EXAMPLE

When we talk about maintaining focus in transition, I like to look at the person of Daniel. It is said of Daniel that, since he was somewhere around the age of 30 up until he was around age 80 he prospered. Remember, this time period spanned seven different political administrations and leaders. We can see that it didn't matter to Daniel whether it was the libertarians in power; or Republicans; or Democrats; or independents. Those around and above Daniel didn't determine whether he prospered. He prospered because he recognized his purpose and understood that, even in transition, that purpose didn't change. Let's look at some passages from the book of Daniel: you'll see in these excerpts how those around Daniel recognize the unique qualities he has received from God—abilities and wisdom that no one else at that time displayed in these ways.

Suddenly the fingers of a man's hand emerged and began writing opposite the lampstand on the plaster of the wall of the king's palace, and the king saw the back of the hand that did the writing. —Daniel 5:5 (NASB)

The queen entered the banquet hall because of the words of the king and his nobles; the queen spoke and said, "O king, live forever! Do not let your thoughts alarm you or your face be pale. There is a man in your kingdom in whom is a spirit of the holy gods; and in the days of your father, illumination, insight and wisdom like the wisdom of the gods were found in him. And King Nebuchadnezzar, your father, your father the king, appointed him chief of the magicians, conjurers, Chaldeans and diviners. This was because an extraordinary spirit, knowledge and insight, interpretation of dreams, explanation of enigmas and solving of difficult problems were found in this Daniel, whom the king named Belshazzar. Let Daniel now be summoned and he will declare the interpretation." —Daniel 5:10-12 (NASB)

Could you imagine how terrifying seeing this hand appear out of the air would be? As everyone is overtaken by fear, the queen remembers Daniel. In this emergency, Daniel is the one known as the man who can interpret enigmatic signs. Sure enough, he comes in, interprets what's on the wall, and what happens comes to pass exactly how he said it would. Darius removes the current king, and himself becomes king.

Let's look at another passage.

It seemed good to Darius to appoint 120 satraps over the kingdom, that they would be in charge of the whole kingdom, and over them three commissioners (of whom Daniel was one), that these satraps might be accountable to them, and that the king might not suffer loss. Then this Daniel began distinguishing himself among the commissioners and satraps because he possessed an extraordinary spirit, and the king planned to appoint him over the entire kingdom. Then the commissioners and satraps began trying to find a ground of accusation against Daniel in regard to government affairs; but they could find no ground of accusation or evidence of corruption, inasmuch as he was faithful, and no negligence or corruption was to be found in him. Then these men said, "We will not find any ground of accusation against this Daniel unless we find it against him with regard to the law of his God." —Daniel 6:1-5 (NASB)

As we read this chapter, we find that the king's original plan gets amended. The three commissioners over the 120 changes into the king appointing Daniel over everything. Daniel is so smart that the king trusts him with his entire kingdom. Remember, this is an Israelite fugitive—he had to learn their culture, their politics, their economy, from scratch. Now, he's running the entire operation! The other men try to find something wrong with Daniel in regard to government affairs. They say to themselves, "The only way we're going to get him is making what he does in his religion illegal. We're going to have to create a law." They created a law that decreed no one had permission to pray to anyone besides the king's gods.

The words used to describe Daniel in this passage are consistent: "extraordinary", "excellent", "spirit of God inside him", "explains and gives insight", "has understanding." These terms weren't spoken by kinsmen or people who shared his faith: only by unbelievers. There's a sense that, everywhere Daniel goes, there's an excellence about him that is impossible to miss.

Imagine what it would be like if, in your business or church, everyone exhibited such excellence that the discussion about them was always, "They have an extraordinary spirit." If this was the case, we wouldn't have to implement a program for church growth: people would be running to church to find out who makes us so excellent. Even in our businesses, though we need to do a good job in marketing, most of what happens is by word of mouth. Daniel had a shining reputation outside of his organization that attracted attention, even though he was in a huge amount of transition.

Maintaining focus in transition has less to do with managing the transition and more to do with managing ourselves. When it comes down to it, we have to admit that we're not very powerful. Our sovereign God is on the throne, and, though we may not like everything He does, we still choose honor Him as God and recognize His sovereignty. He ordains transitions and walks us through them. After all, it was through Daniel that God said, "I raise up one and I put down another" (Daniel 2:21-22).

As Christian leaders, when worldly catastrophe breaks out, we sometimes have a tendency to act like God got kicked off His throne. This isn't the right mindset to have. We have to maintain our confidence in Him. When God places His hand on a man or a woman, it doesn't matter what goes on around him or her; God will cause that woman or that man to be what they were intended to be. He does this by His own hand. My hope is that I can build your faith a bit, so that, in the midst of transition, we maintain a faith that says, "God is in charge, no matter what."

FIVE PRINCIPLES TO MAINTAINING FOCUS

Let's discuss five principles, or five "C"s, that we need in order to become who we're supposed to be.

Commitment—Remaining Faithful

Part of what is ravaging us in today's culture—and in today's church—is the inability to remain committed to anything. We must realize that, rather than tomorrow holding the answers for today, the real preparation for tomorrow's success is in the work we do today. So many people do one of two things: they either walk into the next phase unprepared, or they never get to it at all because of a lack of faithfulness. We don't want to do either.

Here's a bold statement: Where you are right now *is* the will of God for you. That's hard to swallow, because our tendency is to ask, "Lord, where do you want me?" Where you are today is where He wants you. Now, if the Lord moves you somewhere else tomorrow, that's great. But don't waste time praying about where you should be. You should be right where you are. Focus on making this place the best you can. What leads you into the next phase is success in your current phase.

But Daniel made up his mind that he would not defile himself with the king's choice food or with the wine which he drank; so he sought permission from the commander of the officials that he might not defile himself. Now God granted Daniel favor and compassion in the sight of the commander of the officials, and the commander of the officials said to Daniel, "I am afraid of my lord the king, who has appointed

your food and your drink; for why should he see your faces looking more haggard than the youths who are your own age? Then you would make me forfeit my head to the king."
—Daniel 1:8-11 (NASB)

Daniel's conviction is, "I am not going to eat this; I am committed to a particular way of life. I am not going to adjust my beliefs because the culture just changed." This mindset is a transition from living for pleasure to living for purpose. In order for you to maintain your focus in transition, you've got to maintain the level of commitment you've been walking in up to this point. Be faithful. Your faithfulness is seen.

Then, just as they said to Daniel, they will say to you, "You look different. There's a glow about you." This not only helps you maintain focus, but allows you to lead properly in the midst of transition, as well.

Competence—Skills to Contribute

One of the things we've had to work through in our churches is this: commitment does not replace the need for competency. For example, the fact that you really, *really* want to sing on stage doesn't mean, by any account, that we should ever give you a microphone. Those of you who grew up in church have probably been one of these situations where we applaud a poor attempt in order to assuage feelings. Often, we believe commitment equals competence. We don't like sending people out the door just because they're doing a terrible job. So we keep them around and move them throughout different departments. We can't try to replace competency with commitment. The two work together, not in competition. We need to show up, and we need to be good when we show up.

Then at the end of the days which the king had specified for presenting them, the commander of the officials presented them before Nebuchadnezzar. The king talked with them, and out of them all not one was found like Daniel, Hananiah, Mishael and Azariah; so they entered the king's personal service. As for every matter of wisdom and understanding about which the king consulted them, he found them ten times better than all the magicians and conjurers who were in all his realm. —Daniel 1:18-20 (NASB)

The Israelites had been kidnapped from Jerusalem. Their captors drag them across the desert and into Persia. They force them to forget their language, their songs, their music, and to take on an entirely new way of life. Then, these captors have the gall to say, "Now come and serve us, and put a smile on your face." What would you feel? What would you do?

It had to be God that helped Daniel and these other men maintain their focus. Again, not only does Daniel learn a foreign culture—he masters it. He's better at their stuff than they are. He's propagating an excellence they can't fathom. In a land that is not his, before his enemies, this is what he's doing. Only God can make that happen.

Courage—The Heart to Serve

Shadrach, Meshach and Abed-nego replied to the king, "O Nebuchadnezzar, we do not need to give you an answer concerning this matter. If it be so, our God whom we serve is able to deliver us from the furnace of blazing fire; and He will deliver us out of your hand, O king. But even if He does not, let it be known to you, O king, that we are not going to serve your gods or worship the golden image that you have set up." —Daniel 3:16-18 (NASB)

There is such profound courage here. As a people today, we have a serious need for this kind of resolve. The fear sweeping the nation is overwhelming. We need the kind of courage that says, "You're not going to push my heart away from what I know to be true." In the midst of wherever you currently are, ask the Holy Spirit to give you an extra dose courage in your heart.

Compassion—the Love to Meet Needs

"Then Daniel, whose name is Belteshazzar, was appalled for a while as his thoughts alarmed him. The king responded and

said, 'Belteshazzar, do not let the dream or its interpretation alarm you.' Belteshazzar replied, 'My lord, if only the dream applied to those who hate you and its interpretation to your adversaries!' —Daniel 4:19 (NASB)

Daniel is a man who has come through exile, enslavement, and castration, into a different land. He is probably in his mid-fifties at this point. The king's heart has turned, and he's made a new declaration: "We're going to serve Daniel's God." Daniel loves the king. Then, the king has a horrible dream and shares it with Daniel. The interpretation is that seven periods shall pass in which the king will live like an animal because of his pride; but that, one day, he'll be restored.

If Daniel still had a bit of attitude over how he has been treated, he might be jumping up and down to share this news. But Daniel is heartbroken. This level of compassion is powerful. It's the kind of compassion that – here's a novel idea – makes you love your enemies. There is a desperate need for this compassion in our world. Compassion doesn't mean we refrain from calling right right and wrong wrong; but it does mean that, when I decry injustice, I do it in love.

We, as God's ambassadors, are called to love the world. Daniel gives such a strong example for ambassadorship: these are not his kinsmen, but he loves them because this is where he has been sent. Wherever you are, you've been sent there to become an example of what love looks like. Operate in truth; operate in compassion.

Creativity—the Ingenuity to Change

Let's read Daniel 6 again. Darius is king now, and Nebuchadnezzar is gone.

It seemed good to Darius to appoint 120 satraps over the kingdom, that they would be in charge of the whole kingdom, and over them three commissioners (of whom Daniel was one), that these satraps might be accountable to them, and that the king might not suffer loss. Then this Daniel be-

gan distinguishing himself among the commissioners and satraps because he possessed an extraordinary spirit, and the king planned to appoint him over the entire kingdom.
—Daniel 6:1-3 (NASB)

At this point, Daniel is almost 90 years old. We see something fascinating: he's still changing. He's wise enough to accept new leadership. I want to caution younger men and women against getting set into a certain way and not being able to change. You've got to be creative in how you operate in life. You have to have your heart open to what God is doing in this hour—your hour. He does things differently than we do; and sometimes He surprises us.

Daniel was wise enough to embrace new leadership, but he was also excellent enough to get automatic respect. When you move into a new area, you see things others don't see. However, you most likely don't have the credibility to change things right away. If you're mature, you will give it time until you've proven yourself. As you operate in creativity, make sure what you are producing has substance. Spend more time focusing on content than on packaging. What Daniel has in his old age is this serious level of content, that causes the men to say, "We can't find anything wrong with him. He's got it together." Because of that, God promotes him. Make sure you have creativity with content—then you'll have credibility, and credibility will get you somewhere.

If we can be committed, competent, courageous, compassionate and creative, we can weather transitions and demonstrate our abilities to a world that desperately needs to see the hope that we have in Christ.

CLOSING THOUGHTS

What I've asked folks to do, especially leaders, is to spend a little less time studying transitions and more time studying what your purpose ought to be during every transition. What principles will maintain you, regardless of what's happening?

Then, let the transitions come—because they will. Don't get so caught up in the details and the drama of the transition that you lose sight of the stabilizing purpose of God for your life. Let's lean into Him and root our purpose and practices in His truth—in the fact that He's on the throne.

Bishop B. Courtney McBath is the pastor of Calvary Revival Church in Norfolk, Virginia. He is a graduate of MIT and has a Doctorate of Ministry from Providence Bible College and Theological Seminary. In 1998, he founded the Calvary Alliances of Churches and Ministries, an organization that serves pastors and leaders in the U.S., Africa, India, and the Caribbean. Bishop McBath's heart is to see people enjoy a vibrant relationship with Jesus Christ and walk in God's will for their lives. He is married to his wife, Janeen, and has five children and four grandchildren.

chapter 10

MASTERING TRANSITION

/ / / / / / / / / / / / / / / / /

by Dr. Sam Chand

A S HUMAN BEINGS, we're all in transition. We have been in transition in the past, and our futures hold transition. Even after you die, your legacy will still create transitions for others. Transitions can take many different forms—we've all experienced them professionally, educationally, geographically, or between life stages. Moving from one thing to the next is a normal part of our existence.

I wrote about this concept in my book, *Futuring*, about 15 years ago. Over the years, our culture's mindset has shifted in many different areas. Years ago, for example, the average American would hold a single-digit number of jobs over the course of a professional career. Today, the average American young person will have around 20 jobs in his or her lifetime. Why the change? Cultural transition. Most of us grew up thinking that home ownership was the epitome of the American dream. Nowadays, the rental market has grown much bigger, because home ownership isn't necessarily all it's cracked up to be. People do business differently. People buy for different reasons and in different ways—just consider the uptick in on-line sales over the past few years.

In each of these transitions, we discover the need to adapt our practices to the changes happening around us. Best Buy had to amend their sales strategies in order to compete with sites like Amazon.com. Churches, likewise, must alter expectations and outreach methods to the more mobile, tech-connected congregations of today. People used to attend church in person every Sunday; now, two Sundays a month is considered regular attendance.

All this being said, I want to use this chapter to examine how we, as believers, have the ability to adapt to and master each type of transition life offers us.

EIGHT TRANSITIONS

I want to discuss eight transitions everyone has been through, is going through, or will go through at some point in life. The challenge is not only the transition itself, but also determining how to keep moving forward in the midst of it. How do we keep from losing heart and momentum? How do we keep our eyes focused on where we are going? Let's look at each type in turn and explore these concepts.

People

The biggest transition you're going to have, in terms of impact, is new people coming into your life. You will have a need for different people at different levels and stages. The challenge inherent in this transition is discerning with whom to engage, with whom to disengage, and what level of engagement or disengagement you will have with each one. Think of engagement as a continuum: there are some people along that line you could go months without talking to; other people, you can't imagine not being in your life. Think of a person who was very important to you at one time, but not necessarily at this time. Now, think of someone very import-ant to you now that you didn't know 18 months ago. These people will shift depending on the other transitions hap-pening. But what I've found, and what I believe you'll find, is that the people you surround yourself with make the single biggest impact in your life.

Consider these wise words. Do any of them resonate with the People Transitions you've experienced?[9]

- *It is better to be alone than in the wrong company. Tell me who your best friends are, and I will tell you who you are.*

- *If you run with wolves, you will learn how to howl, but if you associate with eagles, you will learn how to soar to great heights.*

- *A mirror reflects a man's face, but what he is really like is shown by the kind of friends he chooses.*

- *The simple but true fact of life is, you become like those with whom you closely associate for the good and the bad. The less you associate with some people, the more your life will improve.*

- *Anytime you tolerate mediocrity in others, it increases your mediocrity.*

- *An important attribute in successful people is their impatience with negative thinking and negative acting people.*

- *As you grow, your associates will change. Some of your friends will not want you to go on. They will want you to stay where they are.*

- *Friends that don't help you climb will want you to crawl.*

- *Your friends will stretch your vision or choke your dream.*

---

9. *Know Your Limits - Then Ignore Them,* by John Mason, Insight Interna-tional, Inc., 1999, pp. 13-14 .

- *Those that don't increase you will eventually decrease you.*

- *Consider this: never receive counsel from unproductive people. Never discuss your problems with someone incapable of contributing to the solution, because those who never succeed themselves are always first to tell you how. Not everyone has a right to speak into your life. You are certain to get the worst of the bargain when you exchange ideas with the wrong person.*

- *Don't follow anyone who's not going anywhere. With some people you spend an evening: with others you invest it. Be careful where you stop to inquire for directions along the road of life.*

With whom you engage, and to what level, will determine your trajectory. If you were to show me your caller ID, I could tell you where you are headed. It's pretty simple. It goes back to what our parents used to say to us when we started hanging around certain new friends: "I don't want you playing with him. He's a bad influence on you." We're not children anymore; so here's my question for you: who in your adult life has permission to say that to you? If you don't give people permission to speak into your life like that, you're headed for trouble. You are where you are today because of somebody.

Pain

The second transition is that of pain. The higher you go, the greater the pains you're going to experience. Everybody wants a big church, but nobody wants to pay the price for a bigger church. Everybody wants to be a CEO, thinking they'll have it easier in the CEO's office; but the reality is, the CEO has the most work and pressure on his plate out of everyone. The higher you go, the harder you're going to work. When you're at the top, you're never off duty.

I know many of us in the church, in business, and in life, aspire to be at the top of the hill. I want to talk you out of that as much as possible. It may seem like the top has only perks, but there's a huge transition we must come to grips with inherent in the climbing. Moving up levels comes with a pain transition.

Places

To explain this transition, I want to offer you a visual illustration. There are two kinds of places. One we call a landscape. The other we call a seascape. Imagine, for a moment, that I am standing on the beach and you are in the ocean. Behind me stands a building—a hotel, maybe. So behind me is the landscape; in front of me is sea. As I am standing here, watching the seascape, how often is it changing? How often is the landscape changing?

We as humans like stability, but we love the ocean. If you ever want to discover new lands in your life, you will have to be willing to lose sight of the shoreline. Everything within us as human beings wants us to move from the uncertain to the certain, from the unknown to the known. When I read my Bible, and look at my personal life, I see that God is always moving us in the opposite direction: from the certain to the uncertain, from the known to the unknown. If you don't make peace with new places like the seascape, you'll stay stuck. After all, that building has been there a hundred years, and never once moved.

How do you keep momentum? Remind yourself, "I was there; but this is where I am going." Everyone wants to say, "I am going to the next level." However, to go to new places, you've got to have the courage it takes to get there. As long as you focus on danger, you will never change. Whenever I am changing, this is a question I ask myself: "What's the worst that can happen?" I face the answer to that question and acknowledge it, but I don't live in the danger zone. Yes, I accept, there are dangers, but if we always focus on them, we will always only make safe decisions. Safe decisions yield nothing of substance; they are simply a rearranging of hotel furniture, and they never lead you anywhere new.

Perspective

We all must learn to think in new ways. How does this happen on a human level? Here's a huge piece of wisdom: Every person needs a coach in their life. The biggest gift a coach gives to you is a different perspective. A coach does not tell you what to do. A coach helps you think at a different level.

My question for you is this: "Who in your life makes you think?" These aren't just going to be the people who agree with you; as you go through changes, you will need to see things differently than you ever have. If you never change perspectives, you'll never become different, better. Who in your life is showing you new perspective?

I have 11 mentors in my life, and I have categorized them according to the different ways in which they speak into me. I wrote about them in my book *Who Moved You Ladder?* Whenever I am faced with a major decision in one area, I ask the appropriate mentor for counsel and feedback. I have a mentor who helps me in marriage. I have people who help me think about business. I have some people help me with my finances. I have people who help me with thinking through what my books look like.

When I was a teenager, my parents were the dumbest people I had ever met. But, as I got older, guess what happened to my parents? They got wiser. Now that they're dead, they're the wisest people I've ever known. Yet their wisdom was not in what they said to me; it was in what they saw. Who shows us? Who asks us questions? Who clarifies the way? Who in your life is giving you the new perspective you need?

Priorities

If you want to be successful, you have to come to the realization that you cannot possibly do everything. When I flew into D.C. on the morning I met with the Renaissance Leadership Network, we flew over the Potomac—that beautiful, wide, slow-moving, lazy river spread out below us. If I wanted that river to move faster, with greater momentum, what would I have to do? Think about it. I would have to narrow it down: concentrate the flow of the water to increase its power. If you want more momentum in your life, you've got to narrow your priorities. Everybody starts in life as a generalist: we attempt to do everything—or perhaps we're told that we need to be able to do everything—and eventually, we become a slow-moving, wide, lazy river. Nobody's really excited about a sluggish river. There's not much momentum, and little focus, when you attempt to do it all. Consider instead the tumbling rapids that so many outdoorsmen eagerly navigate— the challenging thrill and power of concentrated energy.

Here's another example. Light moves to us in its natural way, and we don't think it's very exciting most of the time. However, scientists can harness that same light and turn it into a laser beam that can cut through steel. The power and impact depends on the breadth of its focus.

What are your priorities? If you want to really be successful, narrow your priorities to a few things and do them exceptionally well. To do a few things, you'll first need to the most difficult thing, and that is to say 'no'. Our culture emphasizes saying yes to everything, especially before age 40. You become successful in life by saying, "Yes, I can do that. Yes, I can do that, too. Oh, I don't know anything about it, but I can do it. Yes. Yes. Yes." Somewhere along the way, we have a realization—a midlife crisis, a burnout, something that precipitates us re-evaluating the yes mentality we've always adopted. Success begins to be defined not by all the things we can say yes to, but what we say "no" to. We have to add this word to our vocabulary in order to determine what it really is we want—what our priorities truly are.

Passions

I have different dreams now than I did years ago. My passions have shifted. I will move and cancel a large speaking engagement if, instead, I have an opportunity to go into a modest-sized room and speak with leaders. Why? Because talking with leaders is my passion at this time. What is fueling your passions today? What makes you laugh? What makes you cry? What makes you pound the table? What makes you exuberant? What makes you shout for joy? What just kills your heart? We want to be sensitive to the callings and interests God is laying on our hearts in each new season. Don't fret when these shift or seem to replace one another; it simply means you are being prepared for a new season that requires new dreams.

Ask yourself this fundamental question: "If I didn't have to make money, what would I want to do?" That's what we call the ultimate existential question. Now, you've got your priority. You may need new priorities underneath that, addressing how you'll go about things; but we first want to narrow our focus to those core, key things, and do them really well.

Preparation

The next type of transition is that of preparation. I want to point out a distinct difference between planning and preparation. If you were to ask me, "How long did it take you to prepare what you're sharing in this chapter?" My answer would be, about 35 years. If you were to ask me, conversely, "How long did it take you to plan this content?" I would answer, "A couple of hours." Planning is the specific act, but preparation is something you bring to the table. All of life's preparations—good, bad, joyful, traumatic—have prepared you for where you are right now.

Here's a formula:

Preparation + Opportunity = Success

You may not always have a plan, but opportunities come to those who are prepared. If you are prepared, good things will happen.

Possibilities

I think the biggest transition in my life is being able to dream dreams I haven't dreamed before. This is largely tied to the passion transition but is distinct in that it deals with how big we are willing to dream. A transition in possibilities comes about when I give myself the permission to ask, "What if?"

In the midst of transition, you have the choice whether or not you will stabilize. Our human nature attempts to stabilize the change as quickly as possible. May I suggest, however, that in doing so, we lose the greatest potential? In the midst of a transition, something profound is at play: everything is in flux. You have the freedom and opportunity to make changes. To rise higher. To become better. Something within us tends to hunker down in fear; but, if you give yourself permission to dream a bigger dream, you'll find that the place your biggest dreams are going to come into being is in the middle of transition.

Each of these eight types of transitions will come about in your life, whether individually or in tandem with one another. The important thing to remember is that we want to make the most out of each one. We want to harness the opportunity inherent in each shift. We want to be ahead of and adapt to the curve, not become thrown off by it.

CLOSING THOUGHTS

Keep in mind, as you face transitions, that they are good in nature. Actually, they are wonderful. Every transition and problem is the catalyst that sparked a solution—an answer. Every app on your phone, for instance, is the result of a transitional problem someone saw, addressed, and solved. The world belongs to those who have solutions. Whenever you meet somebody who tells you that they have a problem, listen carefully, and be prepared: you may have the answer. Problem identifiers don't make any money. Problem solvers do.

Begin by truly discovering and embracing how you are uniquely wired. If you don't love people, for instance, don't go into ministry. If you're not passionate about business, don't start one. You have to know yourself; at different times in your life, you will possess different graces for different purposes.

Self-discovery and self-awareness are two different things. Self-discovery can come from people—a motivational speaker, for instance, or the insight of a close friend. Self-awareness, in contrast, is found on the inside: it's being aware of the environments that bring you life, and the environments that take away your joy. The more self-aware you are, the more maturity you can bring into your own life.

Transitions are either healthy or unhealthy. When you're in one, don't be in a hurry to fix the flux you're going through. That season of change—that seascape—is where opportunities lurk. When you're not in transition, and you're around other people going through it, don't offer them easy answers—there are none. People simply need someone beside them who will nonjudgmentally do life with them. That's why people are always the most important piece. Those kinds of people are the ones who become lifelong friends.

Dr. Sam Chand is a leadership architect and consultant whose life vision is helping others succeed. He is a former pastor and college president, , and now serves as President Emeritus of Beulah Heights University. As a Dream Releaser, Dr. Chand serves pastors, ministries, social organizations and businesses through speaking engagements and his books. Dr. Chand shares his life with his wife, Brenda, two daughters, and granddaughters.

chapter 11

MASTERING THE MONEY THING

//////////////////

by Pastor Lee Jenkins

I WAS BORN IN RAISED in the projects of Atlanta. For the first twelve years of my life, I didn't know anything about money. Finances was equivalent to survival, in my mind: finances equaled what you did to make it to the next week. I grew up in a predominantly black area, and the word "wealth," to us, meant that you drove a nice car or had nice clothes. What I wanted growing up was to make a lot of money so I could have those things.

In junior high, I was pretty good at sports. My sights were set on playing professionally, and by the time I graduated high school, I had 30-35 scholarship offers at my fingertips. I chose to attend the University of Tennessee. I was later drafted by the New York Giants. The good news: I achieved my goal. The bad news: I did exactly what I'd been taught to do with money most of my life: I bought stuff, I burned through my money, and I had little to show for everything I had made.

This brought me to a crossroads: I went on a journey. I thought, "There has to be something I don't know about how money works." This curiosity led me into the investment business, where I began work as a stockbroker. Many of the people I chased in my new job had massive amounts of money (after all, you can't make it as a stockbroker chasing broke folks). As I talked to these people, learned about them, I found out that they operated differently than I did. There was a wide gulf in philosophy between millionaires and everyday folks like myself.

I began to study these people with whom I did business: beyond managing their portfolio, I came to know them. After a while, I saw myself prospering—embodying the same lessons I was learning from them. By the time I was 30, I was making over $100,000. By the time I was 40, I was a millionaire. Life was really good at this point. Everything I did seemed to flourish. I was an elder at my church, doing ministry, and had written a couple of books. I travelled around the nation and came home to a 9,000-square-foot home. I thought, "This is perfect. Lord, please don't mess this up for me."

So, what did He do? You guessed it. He messed it up.

God had been nudging my spirit for years—really, since I committed my life to Christ at 18—towards shepherding and pastoring people. I ran from being a pastor all of my adult life—I figured, if I made enough money, God would eventually give up and leave me alone. While He allowed me to make a lot of money, He never left me alone. The 2008 financial crisis was my wakeup call—so many people, including myself, lost wealth and assets in that crash.

The Holy Spirit presented me with a choice. "Do you want to spend the rest of your life investing in the temporal—in things that could be taken away at any moment—or in the eternal work of caring for souls?" My life was shaken. Long story short, on 2012, I launched Eagles Nest Church with a grand total of 15 congregants. Less than five years later, we had grown to over 800 people. The amazing thing was that, the very thing I had been doing for 25 years was the thing God began to utilize in my pastoral life. In the area we began to minister, there lived several CEOs and business owners who never went to church regularly. As these men joined our church, their wives told me, "You're the first pastor my husband has ever gotten up early on Sundays to go listen to, because you speak his language."

I'm reminded of Simon Peter, to whom Jesus said, "I am going to make you a fisher of men." Jesus says to you and me, "I am going to use your skills to win souls for the kingdom." Jesus didn't say, "All that fishing stuff you learned? Throw that away." No. He said, "I am going to use what you've learned for a new, better purpose."

THE STEWARDSHIP PERSPECTIVE

"And you shall remember the Lord your God, for it is He who gives you power to get wealth, that He may establish His covenant which He swore to your fathers, as it is this day.
—Deuteronomy 8:18 (NKJV)

God wouldn't give you the power to do something evil. Unfortunately, many of us in the church have a faulty perspective about money and things, and how they should be used. It is God who gives us power to acquire wealth. The question is, are we using that power? Our focus in this chapter is mastering the money thing: in other words, preventing money from mastering you.

If we're honest with ourselves, most of us are frustrated in this area. We either don't make enough, don't have enough, or have just enough. Most of us desire more than enough (though we may wonder whether this desire is Godly). I find that most people deviate towards one of two extremes when it comes to their perspective on money.

Some people have what I call a poverty mentality: they're scared of money, and believe being poor is a virtue. They may even believe that the poorer you are, the closer you are to God. On the other end of the spectrum is what I call "prosperity theology." Now, nothing is wrong with the word "prosperity." But we can't base your spiritual life on the square footage of our homes. Just because you have stuff doesn't mean you are spiritual. Prosperity theology claims that those with real faith will experience uninterrupted prosperity; but this is not necessarily the truth. Some of the greatest figures in the Bible went through hard times financially, in which God providentially prepared them for greatness.

I believe we should have a perspective that falls in the middle—what I call the "stewardship perspective." The stewardship perspective simply says, "Everything I have belongs to God, and I want to multiply it for His glory." Notice that I didn't say "simply manage it for His glory." A good steward, as we will see in Matthew 25, is a person who manages money for the purpose of *multiplying* it. Are we growing what God has given us?

THE STATE OF THE NATION'S WEALTH

I want to share some statistics with you, to offer a broad perspective on our current national financial situation. Consider the following, as they pertain to cultural—and especially black—finances in America.

- 70% of Americans are living from paycheck to paycheck, regardless of how much money they make. 71% of Americans say debt is making their lives unhappy.

- The median household income for a white family is $67,175, compared to $40,000 for a Latino household and $39,760 for a black household. Blacks are significantly lower in terms of income.

- Blacks own one half of 1% of the nation's wealth. This statistic remains where it was in 1860, on the eve of the Civil War. Though blacks live well in terms of wealth, our percentage of wealth in America hasn't progressed. Wealth, as we're going to talk about, is not what you have on your back, but what you have in the bank: something you can leave for generations.

- 48% of blacks have bad credit, compared to 27% of whites and 34% of Hispanics.

- 1 in 4 African Americans, and just 1 in 6 Hispanics, own stocks, bonds or mutual funds, compared to about half of white workers.

- The average black family passes on zero net financial assets to future generations. Read that one more time. That means most African Americans will not receive an inheritance. Very little is passed down generation to generation. The Bible says,

> A good man leaves an inheritance to his
>   children's children,
> But the wealth of the sinner is stored up for the
>   righteous. —Proverbs 13:22 (NKJV)

- For the most part, the black culture has become a single-generation consumer culture. We make money and use it up in our own generation, with little to nothing left for the next one.

- Blacks give 25% more of their discretionary income to charity than do others.[10] $9 out of every $10 donated by African Americans goes to churches or religious groups. That's a good statistic—that means we're a generous people, and we love our church. So, what better way to get

---

10. *https://www.philanthropy.com/article/How-Americans-Give/188055*

the financial knowledge we need, to learn about wealth, than in the house of God?[11]

FIVE WAYS TO MASTER THE MONEY THING

There are many ways to master your money. These are what I call the five primary ways. They apply to anybody—black, white, Hispanic, Asian, poor, or rich. I believe these five principles can change your life; they changed my life, and the lives of many of the people I worked with for 25 years.

1. You must see money abundantly.

This principle has everything to do with your money perspective. As I said earlier, you might be suffering from a poverty perspective. The definition of "wealth" is having more than enough. Why would you want more than enough? So you can be a blessing to God's kingdom and your family; so you can leave an inheritance to. There are many good things you can do when you have more than enough, but it starts with how you think.

You have probably heard the parable of the talents in Matthew 25, where three stewards receive money from their master. One hides the money, one makes five times the money, and one makes ten times the money. The steward that hid the money *did* manage it, but he was severely criticized by the master. Why? Because he didn't multiply it. He didn't have the right mindset. He didn't see money abundantly. A poverty mentality sees money scarcely: "Maybe being broke is just my lot in life." Proverbs 23:7 says, *"As a man thinketh, so is he."* Wealth-building starts in your mind.

Where is your financial thermostat set? Your temperature is determined by where you set your thermostat. Oprah Winfrey, for instance, has a very high financial thermostat setting. How do I know? Because, if she were worth merely $5 million, she would feel like a failure. You will gravitate

11. *http://www.washingtonpost.com/wp-srv/nation/special/documents/post-kaiser-harvard-race-recession-poll.html?noredirect=on*

towards wherever your thermostat is set. If you're going through hard times financially, don't adjust your thermostat down based on your circumstances. Set it high, and your circumstances will change.

Do you see money as a tool to be used for God's glory? Do you see it as something you have permission to enjoy? Both of these mindsets are Biblical.

2. You must seize money aggressively.

God feeds the birds with worms, but the birds have to go get their food. What you do for a living is the greatest wealth-building tool you have. The happier you are in your job, the more productive you will be. It's essential that you have a seizing mechanism, a strategy, for how you will acquire wealth.

Here are a couple methods by which people seize money.

- *As an employee.* This is how most people go about wealth-making. There's nothing wrong with working for someone else. I know people who makes hundreds of thousands of dollars who don't build as much wealth as people who only make $40,000 or $50,000, because the latter person manages what they have well.

- *As an intrapreneur.* "Intrapreneur" is a word I came up with for someone who works for a company, yet still creates additional income underneath their main role. This may be, for example, in a performance-based capacity: your production level determines your income. As an investment advisor, I was an intrapreneur on 100 percent commission. If I didn't make my sale or get my client, I didn't get paid.

- *As an entrepreneur/self-employed person.* This is someone who turns a skill into a business. He or she is a one-person shop. You could be a school teacher who decides to tutor privately; or you could start your own photography business. This individual takes a core competency and turn it into a consulting practice. By the way, this can also be done part-time in conjunction with other endeavors.

- *As an entrepreneur/business owner.* This option is different from being self-employed because, as a business owner, you hire others to assist in what you do. It's bigger than a one-person show, and you need other folks in order to achieve your vision.

- *As an investor.* This person makes money, but then identifies opportunities into which to multiply that money. Whether it's real estate or business, they discern where they'd like their money to go and grow.

- *Someone who develops multiple streams of income.* Between my wife and me, we have six or seven streams of income. How did we get here? We took our core competencies, what God has called us to do, and said, "Lord, how can we impact your kingdom and make money off of this at the same time?"

Remember when David was facing Goliath. He asked a key question three times before he went to battle with the giant: "How much will be done for the man who kills Goliath?" Yes, his ultimate motivation was to glorify God; but he also needed to know what was in it for him. It's completely possible to fulfill a spiritual assignment and still have a financial reward attached.

3. *You must sow generously.*

God will not bless a stingy person. In my money journey, I've found it essential to establish "finish lines." My wife and I decided we didn't want to keep getting bigger and bigger houses or nicer cars indefinitely. We prayerfully set a line above which we pledged to give everything away—to bless the next generation. Your money can't be all about you. Consider ways to intentionally set aside wealth so that you can bless others

Honor the Lord with your wealth
and with the best part of everything you produce.
Then he will fill your barns with grain,

and your vats will overflow with good wine.
—Proverbs 3:9-10 (NLT)

Many people believe, "If I had more, I would give more." No, actually, you wouldn't. Whatever you do with a little is exactly what you will do with much. The biggest test of how you will handle much is how you handle what you have: that's what determines whether God will trust you with much. What are you doing with what you have right now?

4. You must spend strategically.

The wise have wealth and luxury, but fools spend whatever they get.. —Proverbs 21:20 (NLT)

If you don't tell your money where to go, you're going to be stuck wondering where it went. Here are a couple strategies to help you spend wisely.

- *Live below your means.* I know you've heard this tip your entire life. It's easy to say, but—can we be honest? —it's hard to do. The more we make, the more we want to spend. Resist this temptation, and watch your peace of mind and your financial confidence skyrocket.

- *Develop a spending plan/budget.* Consider this verse from the book of Luke:

  For who would begin construction of a building without first calculating the cost to see if there is enough money to finish it? —Luke 14:28 (NLT)

How can you plan your life without planning your finances? It's essential to know what you have coming in and going out. If you're married, this means you have to work as a team with your spouse. If you're a parent, everyone in the family has to be on the same page. Formulate a specific plan for spending, and be faithful to it.

5. You must save consistently.

Saving has to be a part of your life. You have to be like the ant, who saves in the summer so it has enough in the winter.

Good planning and hard work lead to prosperity,
but hasty shortcuts lead to poverty. —Proverbs 21:5 (NLT)

Christians love get rich quick schemes, probably because we hunger for God to do something miraculous. However, quick fixes, especially financially, aren't indicative of real life and the true wisdom it takes to acquire long-lasting wealth. Here are a few strategies to help you to save consistently.

- *Get out of debt.* When you eliminate debt, you save money. The new slave masters of today are VISA and MasterCard. These companies make a fortune off our nation's financial dysfunction. The Bible says,

  Just as the rich rule the poor,
  so the borrower is servant to the lender.
  —Proverbs 22:7 (TLB)

  If you are always making just the minimum payment to debtors, you'll be paying them for the rest of your life.

- *Get your credit straight.* Though you don't want to borrow a lot of money, you still want the ability to borrow when needed.

- *Pay yourself automatically.* In other words, don't trust yourself. If you have a good track record with yourself, great; but most people don't. Designate this portion to come out of your check automatically.

- *Establish a rainy day fund.* Many people struggle because emergencies come up and they don't have adequate reserves. Make sure you have that peace of mind in savings. Always expect the unexpected.

- *Invest for the long haul.* This strategy refers to participating in the stock market. This is actually how most people's wealth is built. You can no longer rely on your home equity to be the primary source of your wealth, so explore other investment options and choose the path that's best for you.

- *Leave a legacy.* Again, the Bible says, *"A good man leaves an inheritance to his children's children." (Proverbs 13:22).* Part of managing and multiplying wealth is ensuring those who come after you will be set up in a position to do the same.

As a child, I didn't understand that there was another level to finances beyond survival. As I came into wealth as a professional athlete, I didn't know how to handle it, and ended up squandering much of it. As a stockbroker, I learned the wisdom of man-made wealth and picked up helpful principles that are still applicable in my life today. When it comes down to it, though, no one is a better investment advisor than the God who created money in the first place. As we seek to honor Him with our finances, let's prayerfully dedicate everything we have to Him, knowing it's all a gift to be stewarded and multiplied. Let's intentionally set out plans to cultivate wealth, while keeping in mind those whom we can bless through it. Ensuring that you master the money thing in your life will enable you to leave behind a legacy of excellence and responsibility to those who follow after you.

Pastor Lee Jenkins is the founder and senior pastor of Eagles Nest Church in Roswell, Georgia. He is a nationally-recognized businessman, best-selling author, speaker, and financial expert. Churches of all sizes have benefitted from his practical, sound, and humorous presentations of the Gospel. He is happily married to his wife Martica, and has three grown children.

chapter 12

OVERCOMING FEAR IN LEADERSHIP

by Chaplain Barry Black

/////////////////

Go your way; behold, I send you out as lambs among wolves. —Luke 10:3 (NKJV)

W E MUST OVERCOME fear in order to lead. There are real dangers and threats in our world, and we must be ready to encounter and overcome them. For those keeping abreast of politics, social injustice, and the daily news, there may at times be the temptation to become discouraged or to despair. Our Lord reminds us of the predatory nature of our world. We cannot pretend that we're living in *Mister Rogers' Neighborhood*, as many of us tend to do. We must remain watchful and prayerful.

Be sober, be vigilant; because your adversary the devil walks about like a roaring lion, seeking whom he may devour. — 1 Peter 5:8 (NKJV)

Why do we need vigilance? We have an adversary. The opposite of vigilance is naiveté. Joseph was naïve about his brothers before they sold him into slavery. He freely spilled all his dreams to them and gave evil reports about them to his father. You've got to be careful to whom you tell your dreams and about whom you talk. The book of James says,

> *Know this, my beloved brothers: let every person be quick to hear, slow to speak, slow to anger. —James 1:19 (ESV)*

God gave us two ears and one mouth. Particularly as leaders, we must twice as much as we speak. A leader doesn't come in with a bag of tricks and claim to be the solution to every problem. That's not leadership. Leadership is listening, learning, and mobilizing people toward a shared objective.

THE FEAR OF LEADERSHIP

What is fear? It's an unpleasant emotion caused by exposure to danger or expectation of pain. Anyone looking at the world right now knows we are surrounded by danger –terrorism, runaway deficits, poverty, violence, despair...the list goes on. Danger can intimidate us to the point where we don't want to step forward. If you've got a 9' 6" giant like Goliath threatening your life, you're going to be a little intimidated.

We are also surrounded by pain. One of my favorite movies is *Rocky III*, which introduces one of the most interesting characters in movie history, "Clubber" Lang. Someone comes up to Clubber and asks, "What is your prediction for the fight?" Clubber says simply, "Pain." We don't like or desire pain! Fear is a natural reaction to avoid the pain we perceive.

The reality is, many of us are afraid to lead. Like the Israelites in 1 Samuel 17, we see Goliath before us and take on the same posture as they did: "all of Israel trembled and was afraid." From King Saul down to the lowliest enlisted person, the nation stood paralyzed by fear. Then, a teenager too young to be conscripted in the army—a young man anointed by God—was the only one to overcome his fear. David asks the seminal question:

"What will be done for the man who kills this Philistine and removes this disgrace from Israel? Who is this uncircumcised Philistine that he should defy the armies of the living God?"
— 1 Samuel 17:26 (NIV)

David knows his spiritual identity is in God—he knows where his status lies. This is what enables him to overcome his fear. To be the leader God wants you to be, you must have the anointing of God in your life. When you're connected with God—when you pray without ceasing—a miraculous thing happens: you aren't concerned about circumstances or other people. You simply desire to do God's will.

Jesus assures His followers in John 16:33,

These things I have spoken to you, that in Me you may have peace. In the world you will have tribulation; but be of good cheer, I have overcome the world.

Having good cheer in the midst of trouble seems counter-intuitive. Yet Jesus has overcome the world. We have our Promised Land before us, and we possess the ability to have good cheer. That's leading in the midst of fear—knowing that the anointing of God is more powerful than Goliath.

PRINCIPLES FOR OVERCOMING LEADERSHIP

I want to share 10 principles for overcoming fear in leadership, through ten key questions. Each question has a key principle to answer it. Let's explore how to practically overcome fear in our daily lives.

1. What must we trust to overcome our fear of leadership?

In the third year of the reign of Jehoiakim king of Judah, Nebuchadnezzar king of Babylon came to Jerusalem and besieged it. And the Lord delivered Jehoiakim king of Judah into his hand, along with some of the articles from the temple of God. These he carried off to the temple of his god in Babylonia and put in the treasure house of his god. — Daniel 1:1-2 (NIV)

We have to *trust in the unfolding of God's loving providence.* Just as the Israelites had to trust in God when they were handed over to foreign nations, David had to trust that he would survive his battle with Goliath. In both cases, this trust originated from the word God had already given his people.

God assured Israel that they would endure as a nation, though He disciplined them for their disobedience. Likewise, David knew Samuel had anointed him as the future king of Israel. This gave him the courage to go to battle, assured of victory. We must know God's promises and trust the unfolding of His loving providence. As a child of God, do not panic, no matter who is in the White House; no matter the state of your bank account; and no matter the tribulation that surrounds you.

2. What is a critical step in overcoming fear in a challenging time?

Then the king ordered Ashpenaz, chief of his court officials, to bring into the king's service some of the Israelites from the royal family and the nobility—young men without any physical defect, handsome, showing aptitude for every kind of learning, well informed, quick to understand, and qualified to serve in the king's palace. He was to teach them the language and literature of the Babylonians. — Daniel 1:3-4 (NIV)

We must *make preparation to serve.* There are invitations you will never receive if you're not prepared. Daniel had established himself as someone of superior intellect, quick adaptation, and respectful disposition. In the middle of the most traumatic transition in his life, he distinguished himself amongst the captives.

I had a similar experience when I was selected as the 62nd chaplain of the United States Senate. When Dr. Bill Frist, the Republican majority leader, announced my election, he said, "Admiral Black has two earned doctorates." Although I had been competing against 99 other clergypersons, I was the only one with this achievement. How did I accomplish it? As I like to say, life is hard by the yard, but a cinch by the inch. You must always be working on something. Be a lifelong and passionate learner; people will notice your drive.

I completed three master's degrees during my period of preparation, including a master's in management from Salve Regina University. Ninety % of the questions Dr. Frist asked me were related to leadership and management. I was ready. When he asked, "Admiral, what in your opinion is the difference between leadership and management?" I started quoting all the information I had learned—leaders and thinkers and principles—just off the top of my head. To overcome the fear of leadership, you must make great preparation to serve.

Jesus had a three-year ministry, for which He prepared 30 years. Moses spent 40 years in the backside of the desert before he saw the burning bush. Always keep working. Always keep preparing for what God has for you.

3. How can we best protect ourselves as we lead in dangerous times?

But Daniel resolved not to defile himself with the royal food and wine, and he asked the chief official for permission not to defile himself this way. —Daniel 1:8 (NIV)

Daniel knew the eyes of the nation were on him. More importantly, he knew God was watching. He had a responsibility to remain faithful. So he set Biblical parameters for himself, to keep him from crossing lines he did not want to cross.

If you're going to lead without fear, *make a commitment not to defile yourself*. Somebody may always be listening in, watching how you speak and act. Every action and word you release as a leader has the potential of coming back to haunt you. Never say anything in private that you would not want publicly broadcasted.

I consider every phone I pick up to be taped. Haters will try to set me up. I have to protect myself. Make a commitment to integrity so that the devil doesn't derail God's plan for your life.

4. What shield does God provide for leaders with integrity?

Surely, Lord, you bless the righteous; you surround them with your favor as with a shield. —Psalm 5:12 (NIV)

When your ways please the Lord, He makes even your enemies at peace with you. That's why we don't have to be paranoid. God has our backs. If we belong to Him, he works all things for His glory and our good.

I want to share a story that illustrates this. I once had someone in a work context say to me, "First of all, I don't like you."

I replied, "Thank you. That's good. You're candid. Some people would've kept that to themselves, but I appreciate you letting me know where I stand."

He said, "One day, I am going to be sitting on a promotion board, and your name is going to come up. I just want you to know right now that you're dead in the water. You don't stand a chance."

I replied, "I appreciate you telling me that. When I see your name on the promotion board, I will know that you're not a thumbs up for me."

Years went by after this exchange. The promotion board eventually met, and this guy happened to be at the same place he'd been when he threatened me. When I received my second star as an admiral, take a guess who had to come and work for me. To be honest, I was ecstatic when I heard the news. This same man was slotted to be my employee. But I heard the Holy Spirit say, "Don't you lay a hand on him. Let him be. Treat him with kindness."

That's what I did. The man came to work for me. Nine months passed. One day, he came into my office with tears streaming down his face. He fell onto his knees, and said, "You're killing me. Why are you so kind to me? You're driving me crazy. Why?"

I had to be honest. "Well," I said, "if you really want to know the truth, it's not because I want to be kind. The Holy Ghost told me not to touch you, brother; and you'd better hope he keeps on telling me that."

Favor isn't "fair." God blesses us beyond what we could ever deserve. He is a shield around His righteous ones; and He asks that we act with that same grace towards others.

5. *What threats must we resist in leadership?*

Shadrach, Meshach and Abednego replied to him, "King Nebuchadnezzar, we do not need to defend ourselves before you in this matter." —Daniel 3:16 (NIV)

When I overcome the fear of leadership, *I make an unconditional commitment to integrity.* Integrity refuses to be intimidated by the world's threats. What Shadrach, Meshach, and Abednego understood was the ultimate purpose of their lives—God's glory. Not popularity, acceptance, or power. This life is about God—not us.

When Goliath threatened David, David's integrity refused to be coerced out of what was right.

And the Philistine said to David, "Come to me, and I will give your flesh to the birds of the air and the beasts of the field!" Then David said to the Philistine, "You come to me with a sword, a spear, and a shield, but I come to you in the name of the Lord of Hosts, the God of the armies of Israel, whom you have reviled. This day will the Lord deliver you into my hand. And I will strike you down and cut off your head. Then I will give the corpses of the Philistine camp this day to the birds of the air and to the beasts of the earth so that all the earth may know that there is a God in Israel." –1 Samuel 17:44-46 (NKJV)

Your unconditional commitment to integrity is well-invested, in a God that has the ultimate victory. He is the reason we confidently resist the threats of the world.

6. What faith must we cultivate?

If we're thrown into the blazing furnace, *our faith must be that the God we serve is able to deliver us.* Faith is believing God can. The Bible is clear on this point: we are not in for an easy ride as followers of Christ.

> *Yea, and all that will live godly in Christ Jesus shall suffer persecution.— 2 Timothy 3:12 (KJV)*

The question is not if we will suffer persecution, but when. This is why it's critical to remain aware of what is happening around us. We must cultivate a faith able to stand up to reality: a faith that says, "Regardless of my circumstances, I believe my God is able to deliver me." Professing that God *can* deliver us means also professing that He may *choose not to* deliver us. Like Shadrach, Meshach, and Abednego, we must realize His ways are higher than ours; the outcomes we desire may not always be His plan. This leads us to our next point.

7. What commitment must we maintain?

> *Though he slay me, yet will I hope in him; I will surely defend my ways to his face. —Job 13:15 (NIV)*

Remain committed to God, regardless of the outcome. We need a "...but, if not..." mindset. "He can deliver me; but if not, I still trust Him. I will bless Him with my dying breath. Though He slay me, hallelujah, yet will I trust in Him." This commitment displays a worship of God above our comfort, our wishes, and even our lives. Leadership requires that we see God as the ultimate purpose, and forego our own purposes to yield to Him. This is the only way to lead without fear.

8. Where can we find unexpected freedom?

Your freedom is found in *choosing how you respond to unavoidable challenges.* Seneca said, "They can kill me, but they cannot harm me."[12] He was mirroring what Paul says in Philippians 1:21: "to die is gain." Who believes that? Those who have a different perspective of their trials; those with unexpected freedom.

Consider Jesus on the cross. Another man would have adopted a victim mentality—a spirit of defeat. Not Jesus. He remained in charge of Himself—and everything—as He breathed his last breaths. He said, "Father, forgive them. I choose how I will handle this, for they know not what they do. I choose how I will die. I choose how I will respond. And just to let hell know, they should turn out the lights, because the party is over. *Tetelestai*! It is finished!"

What better picture is there of leading without fear? Regardless of his challenges, Jesus grasped an unexpected freedom. In doing so, He made the way for us to do the same.

9. What choice can we always make in spite of life's circumstances?

Suddenly an angel of the Lord appeared and a light shone in the cell. He struck Peter on the side and woke him up. "Quick, get up!" he said, and the chains fell off Peter's wrists. — Acts 12:7 (NIV)

The principle here is that we must *choose an exemplary response to life's unavoidable tragedies.* Peter has been scheduled for execution. An angel comes to release him. What is Peter doing at this moment? Sleeping! Would you be able to sleep the night before your execution? Or would you be pacing your cell—fretful, worried, begging God for deliverance? We see Peter making a choice. He thinks, "Since they're going to kill me tomorrow, I might as well get a good night's sleep." Again, this goes back to knowing God is in control.

12. *Discourses* (Books 3 and 4), Epictetus. Courier Corporation, 2012, p. 49

10. What fellowships can bring sweetness to our lives in dangerous times?

Find fellowship, with Jesus and others, during fiery trials. Paul said,

> *... that I may know him, and the power of his resurrection, and the fellowship of his sufferings, becoming conformed unto his death. —Philippians 3:10 (ASV)*

We can overcome the fear to lead because of Jesus's promise that he will never leave or forsake us. God is in charge of His world. Trust His providence. Make a commitment not to defile yourself. Don't be intimidated by the threats. Find freedom in life's flames. God has given you the choice of how you will respond.

Overcoming the fear to lead is anchored in trusting and yielding ourselves wholly to our God. David trusted God in the face of Goliath. Shadrach, Meshach, and Abednego trusted Him in the face of the furnace. Peter trusted him at the brink of execution. Jesus trusted Him in the middle of His crucifixion. What fears haunt your spirit as you make preparations to be a Godly leader? Surrender these fears to God, and let Him revive your trust in His good, all-powerful, and perfect love.

Chaplain Barry Black is the 62nd Chaplain of the United States Senate. He served for over 27 years in the US Navy Chaplain Corps, and has received several distinguished leadership awards for his service. Chaplain Black holds three Master of Arts degrees and two doctorates. He is also a published author. He is happily married to his wife, Brenda, and they have three sons.

chapter 13

ADAPTING TO GENERATIONAL CHANGE

///////////////

by Pastor Alphonso R. Bernard

IN MY LIFE, I have found change to be the only constant. If we don't know how to change, we will be left behind. The younger generation of today presents a great challenge in terms of changing worldview. Their buying patterns are different. Their thinking is different. What drives them is different. In fact, millennials are redefining how organizations operate in a profound way. Businesses, churches, and other entities are shifting the way they operate and interact with our society. To insist on continuing in the old systems is to lose out on impacting a generation. We must understand new thought patterns if we want to effectively dialogue with those who espouse them.

People are reinventing themselves—either because they haven't discovered who they are yet, or because they feel pressured to keep up with the world around them. Change is good, depending on what it is you're changing. For the new generation, perhaps the most fundamental thing being rede-fined is their set of values.

Millennials are distinguishing between religion and spiritual-ity. They desire to break away from rules and boundaries, rather than conform to expectations. This is fascinating because, when they come full circle, they actually end up establishing rules, or-der and boundaries of their own. We realize that rules protect a society; freedom requires boundaries in order to be preserved. For instance, If someone gets out of debt and achieves financial freedom, that person better have rules in place to prevent getting back into debt. Often, we misunderstand freedom as the ability to do whatever we want. This is not the case.

As we study generational changes in perspective, we'll see that there are pros and cons to each of "side". Baby Boomers have much to impart to youth; and millennials have refreshing values that benefit society, as well. Let's take an in-depth look at how perspectives on work, church, and social interactions have shifted in recent years.

GENERATIONAL SHIFTS: MILLENNIALS VS. BABY BOOMERS

At one time, the work world, and the employment mindset, centered around one thing: the paycheck. Primarily, Baby Boomers' desire was to get paid. While they cared about their work, their main motivation was increasing their value in the marketplace, in order to increase their salaries. They were committed to twenty or thirty years at the same company, working the traditional 9 to 5 shift. Millennials, however, are not driven in terms of a what they make (though, of course, they do want to get paid). They are more concerned with pur-pose. They desire to work for an organization with an admira-ble mission. If this opportunity happens to come with a small-er paycheck, most millennials consider it a worthwhile trade. This perspective shift prioritizes job satisfaction over climb-ing into a particular tax bracket; personal development in the workplace over financial achievement.

Where Baby Boomers accept orders willingly, and even understood micromanagement to a certain degree, the younger generation balks at this style of leadership. Rather than a "boss," they desire a coach—someone who understands and speaks into them. While Baby Boomers were accustomed to the annual review, millennials' communication style is a continuous conversation. They require constant evaluation, without which they feel ignored or confused about their status in the company.

Millennials don't see work as merely a job to clock in and out of daily. For them, work is representative of their life. They are highly focused on atmosphere and purpose. Young people are asking the question, "Does this organization give me the opportunity to do what I love every day?" If not, nearly any other consideration is viable to be changed in order to get to that place. In this sense, they may be considered more "high maintenance" than Boomers, who on the whole are more willing to do work with less feedback and with fewer questions asked.

If we translate these workplace perspectives into the church environment, you can probably guess some of the results. In fact, you've probably witnessed contrasts amongst generations in your church. Baby Boomers are accustomed to certain values, and are committed to consistent church attendance. But trends and mindsets have shifted with Millennials.

I am a Baby Boomer. When I gave my life to Christ, I understood my relationship with God as one of obedience. I knew I needed to conform my life to the Biblical and church standards set before me: to a new lordship. Mention conformity to millennials, however, and you'll probably get an offended expression in return. Young people, as a whole, don't want to hear about how they must fit their lifestyle into the requirements of the church; they want to know how the church fits into their lifestyle. Millennials want to feel connected with others and have a good experience when they come to church. Think about it: nowadays, we call this portion of the service the "worship experience." You can have a great product—a theologically rich sermon, authentic worship, and loving congregants—but if the experience doesn't challenge and engage millennials, they'll go somewhere else.

This may seem like a downside to the new way of thinking; and indeed, one may prefer the commitment of Boomers. Interestingly enough, the comparison of weaknesses and strengths brings up another generational contrast. Millennials don't like to focus on their weaknesses. They prefer to emphasize what they've done well. This means many young church members don't want to hear about sin. They would much rather hear about how good they are and how God is going to bless their socks off. Why? Because these sentiments don't make a demand for individual change.

These shifts may seem drastic. It's common to hear each generation comment about how different, and inferior, the other's perspective is. However, if we look back to the 1960s, we see much of the same thing happening at that time. The youth of that day emphasized antiestablishment thinking; the older generations said many of the same things about the youth. We see that history repeats itself, albeit in slightly different colors. What's important to understand is not which perspective is better, but rather, how to relate to and converse effectively with people who hold different viewpoints.

Now, by no means does this necessitate that we water down or avoid sharing the everlasting truths of the Gospel. The purpose of studying shifts is not to compromise truth, but to find ways of effectively communicating with all generations. After all, if we refuse to change our *methods* of evangelism and discipleship, we lose the opportunity to converse with people who need to hear about Christ. We cannot deal with life the way we would like it to be. We have to deal with life the way it is. Solomon said this so clearly in Ecclesiastes 4. We have to know and understand how the world works, and then proceed to work *within* the system, without becoming *of* the system.

ADAPTING TO CHANGES IN PERSPECTIVE

How do we understand, interact with, and influence today's generation in the church, specifically? I'd like to offer some suggestions based off my discoveries in ministry.

Firstly, we must ensure we are connecting with our *congregants*. In our church, I tell my entire staff that the experience we offer begins on the sidewalk, before people get inside the gate. From the parking lot until the final song, we want to offer the best (and most meaningful) experience possible. Because this generation has a grand desire for purpose, I've taught my staff the difference between a task and a purpose—you cannot have one without the other. For instance, my purpose is to make people feel warm and welcome and safe inside our walls. If I perform the task of seating them in a cold, impersonal way that makes them feel like cattle instead of people, I will have fulfilled my task, while failing at my purpose. If we're so focused on fulfilling tasks that we lose sight of our purpose, people will quickly catch on to that.

Our church has also rethought our small group structure, in order to create an environment where we monitor growth, and interact, more frequently. Remember, the youth of want ongoing communication. Personally, I'm huge on customer service. I wanted to see how other successful companies train their staff. I met with companies like American Express and Disney, who are renowned for their service. This allowed me to gain immense insights. We led our team in extensive training by following the model of the Disney corporation. No matter what capacity they serve in, my staff are required to go through this training course, and demonstrate to leadership how they interact with congregants during the service. Lovingly serving others is essential. In the end, it's all about the people.

After we completed our training with our team at the time, I decided to take them to Disney. It was incredible. The leaders at Disney approached me and said, "Your people know more about our model than we do! We need to step up." That's what effective service looks like.

This story leads into the next thing I want to examine: the other side of the coin, if you will. We as churches must connect with our *staff* in light of generationally changing perspectives. We must ensure the health of our culture—and the satisfaction of our employees—is at an all-time high. I believe the difference lies in the space between compliance and commitment.[13] When people do everything you require of them, that is compliance; but just because people comply doesn't mean they are committed. You must have a process to move team members from compliance to commitment. Realizing this, we began to rethink the way we interacted with our staff.

As we've examined, this new generation desires ongoing conversation. Staff assessments have to occur more frequently. We must develop lines of communication between every level of leadership, from executives down to the lowest staff rung. Everyone has to be engaged in this conversation in order for people to feel heard, valued, and involved in that admirable mission that's so essential. This interactive culture will not emerge on its own; you must create it.

Our church holds staff meetings every other month. We assemble the entire team and ask for everyone to contribute. At one such meeting, I handed out surveys, asking my staff to demonstrate that they could articulate our brand identity. I also asked them to list strengths, weaknesses, and proposed solutions for the company. I told them, "Don't come to me with criticism if you don't have a solution." Most of my colleagues in ministry would never hand out such a survey, because it's human nature not to want to know our weaknesses. Pride gets in the way—we are terrified to discover the truths within our congregation or our staff. For this reason, most churches have a secret, revolving door that, unfortunately, remains

13. *https://www.forbes.com/sites/rodgerdeanduncan/2014/01/01/compli-ance-and-commitment-feel-the-heat-see-the-light/#2ee18017466b*

unexplored and unevaluated. Feedback is critical for ongoing success—you have to know how you are doing, in all areas, to know what needs to be changed or kept. Because of this survey, we received wonderful expressions and constructive criticism from our staff. Their answers allowed me to realize that, while we had been successfully creating community amongst our members, we were failing in creating community amongst our staff. We had to tweak our methods.

Change is the essence of maturation. We will never change until we stop making excuses and face the truth. After all, truth is what brings the conviction necessary for change. Because of this, all truth is confrontational. We must take a long, hard look at what things we need to keep, and what things we need to change.

KNOWING WHAT TO CHANGE AND WHAT TO KEEP

How do we discern which organizational elements we need to keep, and which we should allow to evolve with the times? This may seem daunting at first, considering the numerous elements inherent in church leadership. Let's start with a simple question. Surprisingly, it's not "How do we need to change?" Rather, it's this one:

"Why do we exist?"

You absolutely have to begin with your identity as an organization in order to have longevity. In my ministry experience, longevity is the ability to manage continuity and change simultaneously. Let's break each of concepts these down.

Let's first explore continuity—things that need to stay the same. Continuity is an uninterrupted succession and flow in the experience we provide. I personally have been part of establishing a 20-year succession plan for our church. I created Christian Cultural Center, but it's going to take a team of people to lead it into the future after I am gone. We have a years-long process laid out, in which transition amongst leaders is going to take place. I see too many people in leadership working in a manner that assumes they will die "in office." Many times, mentorships are not cultivated, and knowledge and wisdom are not passed on, with enough time to ensure a smooth and successful hand-off of the baton. We need to have leaders who are holding the baton while the successor is also holding the baton. This ensures continuity will be maintained.

What is the essence of that baton? Continuity also requires systems and structures to be put into place and maintained. As we've discovered, freedom requires rules. For Christian Cultural Center, I created a set of four timeless fundamentals upon which our ministry is built. They are:

1. Core values
2. Core purposes
3. A relentless drive for progress
4. Strength beyond the presence of any one individual

These four fundamentals are the essentials that guide our organization's thoughts and actions. They form the foundation of our ministry, and they will ensure that Christian Cultural Center endures into the future, regardless of the methods we will inevitably change along the way.

Now, let's discuss things that should adapt with time. Change can be defined as transition from one form, state, style, method, place, or level, to another. Just as we experience life in different stages, organizations develop in the same manner. In order to manage continuity and change effectively, you must know what to change. If you don't—if you accidentally change what you should continue (the fundamentals), you will lose your identity. If you continue what you should change—methods of delivery, business practices, operating strategies—you will undermine your success. In short, your core purpose is what ultimately endures; then, you must continually develop new methods by which to carry out that purpose.

The shifting world makes demands on us. First and foremost, it demands that we provide clear identification of who we are, what we do, and what our purpose is. Vision determines our trajectory, rather than method. I believe the one thing that is the lifeblood of any organization, whether church, business, or ministry, is *creativity*. Do not ever lose your creativity; it is the thing that gives birth to solutions and change. Be ever creative in your methods, and ever faithful in your identity.

SPEAKING THE WORLD'S LANGUAGE

There's a wonderful passage in Ecclesiastes 9, in which Solomon reflects on and compares wisdom and folly. He writes,

> *"Here is another bit of wisdom that has impressed me as I have watched the way our world works." —Ecclesiastes 9:13 (NLT)*

The important phrase here is, *"the way our world works."* Ecclesiastes is written from the perspective of a man who took the time to truly observe our world. Solomon's ultimate conclusion was that all is vanity—there is nothing more important than the love of God. Too often, Christians have limited ourselves to speaking in a language that only other Christians understand. We think within an insulated context. We fail to speak the language of the world because we're afraid of, or turned off by, it. This is something we need to improve on, because in this world, whoever controls the language controls the conversation.

As an example of this principle, consider the recent developments in the sexual identity conversation happening in America. The terms used to define homosexual relationships have transitioned several times: from "gay marriage," to "same-sex union," to "marriage equality." When that language came onto the scene, it successfully appealed to the mainstream culture. The moment you introduce the word "equality," you change the game: everybody wants equality, right? In changing the language, same-sex advocate groups achieved a broader appeal, and forwarded their movement. It's true across the boards—in politics, civil rights, and everyday discussions – whoever controls the language controls the conversation.

Christians, to a certain degree, have remained at a loss about how to effectively articulate biblical truths to the world. At one time, we were criticized for being worldly when we were too culturally savvy. But what happens on the opposite side of the spectrum—when we cannot interact with the world at all? If we're completely dismissed by this world, the salt loses its flavor. For this reason, I make it my business to discover, study, and speak the language of the world—to gain understanding for the ultimate purpose of better serving, helping, engaging, strengthening, and encouraging others. After all, our mission is to go and make disciples. How can we do this if we cannot communicate effectively?

Learning to speak the language of the world, of course, never means compromising the Biblical truths we believe. Rather, it stems from a discernment that recognizes cultural shifts and adapts to meet the changing needs of the world. Show the world that you see, understand, and care about them, and you're guaranteed to provide a ministry experience that has them coming back, consistently, for more.

Pastor Alphonso R. Bernard Sr. is the senior founder of Christian Cultural Center in Brooklyn, New York. He is the president of the Council of Churches in New York City, and part of the New York City Economic Development Cooperation. Pastor Bernard also founded the Cultural Arts Academy Charter School, which is a comprehensive educational alternative. He serves alongside his wife, Karen, and they have several beloved children.

chapter 14

GIVE AND TAKE: THE DEVELOPMENT STAGES OF A LEADER

///////////////////

by Bishop Derek Grier

M ANY OF US are familiar with the Marlo Thomas quote, "There are two kinds of people in the world: givers and takers. The takers eat well, but the givers sleep well."[14] Today, we're going to focus, in part, on material created by a professor in organizational psychology, named Adam Grant, that addresses the different kinds of people in any organization. Based off of his findings, we'll examine the different categories of behavioral and participation styles that people fall into, and how these stages progress to the place of leadership God desires for all believers to reach.

---

14. Quoted by Frederick Cookinham, *The Age of Rand: Imagining An Objectivist Future World,* iUniverse, June 2, 2005, p. 104.

Adam Grant is a wonder boy. He was the youngest tenured professor at Wharton School of Business, and the highest-rated professor in the school. He is well-celebrated across the globe for his insight and contributions to this field. Grant divides the world into the same two groups as stated above, but adds a third category. He believes that there are givers, takers, and matchers.

THE THREE BEHAVIORAL STYLES

We all give and take in life. That's simply the way that humans operate. The way we are identified, however, is according which one of these behaviors we exhibit the majority of the time. Let's outline each of these categories in more detail.

Givers

Givers search for opportunities to help others. They constantly ask the question, "What can I do for you?" This may be surprising, but exhaustive studies show that givers tend to be the worst performers. This is because they help others more than others help them. Givers fall behind and, at their worst, end up burned out because of this. Here is the twist: while givers tend to be the worst in output, they also possess the highest outli-ers—some of the best results.

Having one giver on your team does not automatically result in an explosion of generosity; in other words, sickness is contagious, but health is not. When givers begin to feel that they're surrounded by wolves—takers—they will ask, "Why should I continue to contribute like a sheep?" For this reason, takers are the most influential members of an organization.

Takers

Takers ask a different question. In every environment they enter, particularly professional ones, takers ask, "What can you do for me?" Studies show that the negative impact of a taker on a team is double or triple the positive impact of a giver. Adam Grant puts it this way: one bad apple spoils a barrel, but one good egg does not make a dozen.[15] Takers cause givers to stop helping, and bring down the entire team. They are shooting stars that rise quickly but fall just as fast. This fall typically happens at the hands of a matcher.

Matchers

The largest group of people are the matchers. This is the "tit-for-tat" group. Their guiding principle is, "If you do it for me, I'll do it for you." Matchers reciprocate, and expect reciprocity, in their relationships. They are concerned about balance and justice, and feel it's their life's calling to make sure these scales are balanced.

THE TOXICITY OF TAKERS

Consider this passage from the Biblical account of the early church:

> *But a certain man named Ananias, with Sapphira his wife, sold a possession. And he kept back part of the proceeds, his wife also being aware of it, and brought a certain part and laid it at the apostles' feet.* —Acts 5:1-2 (NKJV)

Ananias contributed, but held back. Underneath his veneer of generosity, Ananias was a taker. He was probably trying to please the crowd, or, perhaps, buy a leadership position. Ananias and Sapphira wanted the benefits of church membership without making the same investment as everyone else did. We all know what happened next. Peter had to draw a line.

> *Now it was about three hours later when his wife came in, not knowing what had happened. And Peter answered her, "Tell me whether you sold the land for so much?"*
>
> *She said, "Yes, for so much."*
>
> *Then Peter said to her, "How is it that you have agreed together to test the Spirit of the Lord? Look, the feet of those*

---

15. https://slate.com/business/2014/05/adam-grants-give-and-take-atheory-that-says-generous-people-do-better-at-work-than-selfish-ones.html

who have buried your husband are at the door, and they will carry you out."

Then immediately she fell down at his feet and breathed her last. And the young men came in and found her dead, and

carrying her out, buried her by her husband.

So great fear came upon all the church and upon all who heard these things. —Acts 5:7-11 (NKJV)

Why was God so severe? Think about this for a moment. Dealing with takers can be difficult. Not dealing with them is far worse. The Holy Spirit disciplined Ananias and Sapphira in this manner because He had to protect the church from their influence.

As a leader, you must protect your team. A bad apple has far greater impact than a good one. Sometimes, you must deal aggressively with takers in order to maintain a healthy environment in your organization. Ask yourself this: As a leader, is your primary goal to be liked, or to be respected? We all tend to respond, "respect." In reality, though, we're often more concerned with how others feel towards us than with whether we are doing the right thing.

Cancer cannot be coddled in your team. It must be killed. As believers, we carry out lives of mercy, grace, and love; but we see in Acts that, even in this environment, the Holy Spirit deals with takers. As difficult as this was for Peter, he knew that leadership is not a title; it is an example.

For me, this is sometimes the hardest thing to do as a pastor. I love folks. For the sake of the big picture, I must deal with toxic attitudes and mindsets. I am not a good leader if I ignore them; in fact, I will bring everyone down. Reduction is not always a bad thing; many times, it makes you healthier.

But without faith it is impossible to please Him, for he who comes to God must believe that He is, and that He is a rewarder of those who diligently seek Him. —Hebrews 11:6 (NKJV)

God is the CEO of the universe. This verse lays out His executive management style. God's kingdom is based on the ontological fact that He exists. Secondarily, it is built on the fact that God is a rewarder. If you are rewarded, it means you are being celebrated. We are wired to accomplish, to bring pleasure, and to be rewarded. Likewise, God is by nature a rewarder.

As a leader, what you celebrate (and ignore) cultivates your department's culture. I have learned to look for opportunities to celebrate people when they get things right. What behaviors do you reward? Who gets 'Employee of the Month'? People will watch this. What the CEO rewards gets done; what he corrects ceases.

A SELF-ASSESSMENT

There is therefore now no condemnation for those who are in Christ Jesus. As you reflect on the following passages, consider which group you may fit into today. Keep in mind that, in our work lives, we may fall into a different category than we do in our personal lives. The following are passages describing each behavioral type.

Takers

Takers have a distinctive signature: they like to get more than they give. They tilt reciprocity in their own favor, putting their own interests ahead of others' needs. Takers believe that the world is a competitive, dog-eat-dog place. They feel that to succeed, they need to be better than others. To prove their competence, they self-promote and make sure they get plenty of credit for their efforts. Garden-variety takers aren't cruel necessarily or cutthroat; they're just cautious and self-protective. "If I don't look out for myself first," takers think, "no one will."[16]

---

16. Popova, Maria (2013). "Givers, Takers, and Matchers: The Surprising Psychology of Success." Brain Pickings, *https://www.brainpickings.*

Givers

In the workplace, givers are a relatively rare breed. They tilt reciprocity in the other direction, preferring to give more than they get. Whereas takers tend to be self-focused, evaluating what other people can offer them, givers are other-focused, paying more attention to what other people need from them. These preferences aren't about money: givers and takers aren't distinguished by how much they donate to charity or the compensation that they command from their employers. Rather, givers and takers differ in their attitudes and actions toward other people. If you're a taker, you help others strategically, when the benefits to you outweigh the personal costs.[17]

Matchers

Matchers operate on the principle of fairness: when they help others, they protect themselves by seeking reciprocity. If you're a matcher, you believe in tit for tat, and your relationships are governed by even exchanges of favors.[18]

SUMMARY

Givers, takers, and matchers all can—and do—achieve success. But there's something distinctive that happens when givers succeed: it spreads and cascades. When takers win, there's usually someone else who loses. Research shows that people tend to envy successful takers and look for ways to knock them down a notch. In contrast, when [givers] win, people are rooting for them and supporting them, rather than gunning for them.

THE FOUR PARTICIPATION STYLES

Once your team reduced to only givers and matchers, Dr. Sam Chand, a celebrated leadership expert, still divides people into at least four different participation styles.

---

org/2013/04/10/adam-grant-give-and-take/
17. Ibid.
18. Ibid.

Then the children of Israel journeyed from Rameses to Succoth, about six hundred thousand men on foot, besides children. —Exodus 12:37 (NKJV)

Moses led multiple types of people, with a myriad of motivations. Likewise, as your organization grows, you will encounter and engage with all different types of people. Let's examine four of these groups and their characteristics.

Wanderers

Wanderers don't see the organization's vision, and they also don't particularly care about it. They happen to be present, out of convenience's sake, but aren't invested in the journey. Only God can help this group develop out of their apathy.

Behold, you have driven me today away from the ground, and from your face I shall be hidden. I shall be a fugitive and a wanderer on the earth, and whoever finds me will kill me. —Genesis 4:14 (ESV)

Cain, a man who murdered his brother, is voicing concern about people hurting him. Cain's apathy for Abel seems almost sociopathic. He displays no repentance. We see that Cain was a wanderer. He didn't seem to deeply care about God or his belated brother Abel. He only cared about himself.

Followers

Followers see the vision, but don't pursue it on their own initiative. They have to be directed. These people say things such as, "This is just the way I am. I don't care what you say." As leaders, we must to recognize that there is nothing we can do about followers, either. They must be moved by the Spirit to mature.

Aaron, the high priest in the Old Testament, fell into this group. He only led with excellence as long as his brother, Moses, was with him.

And Moses said to Aaron, "What did this people do to you that you have brought so great a sin upon them?"

So Aaron said, "Do not let the anger of my lord become hot. You know the people, that they are set on evil. For they said to me, 'Make us gods that shall go before us; as for this Moses, the man who brought us out of the land of Egypt, we do not know what has become of him.' And I said to them, 'Whoever has any gold, let them break it off.' So they gave it to me, and I cast it into the fire, and this calf came out." —Exodus 32:21-25 (NKJV)

Moses went up the mountain, talked to God, received the Ten Commandments, came back down, and found everybody throwing a huge, pagan party. Aaron didn't accept responsibility. The high priest blamed the people for what happened. We see that Aaron was an effective leader only as long as Moses didn't spend too much time on the mountain.

Some people must to be supervised: they're not executive material. If you put someone like this on top, you will run into trouble. I have made mid-level team members into executives, and encountered huge problems as a result. Followers placed into leadership cause frustration. I am learning to embrace mid-level people as essential to the cause of an organization, without putting them into executive positions.

Achievers

The third group is comprised of achievers. This is the category toward which I naturally gravitate; if it wasn't for God, I wouldn't move from this spot. Achievers are gripped by the vision, and intrinsically motivated to take action.

So Ahab sent for all the children of Israel, and gathered the prophets together on Mount Carmel. And Elijah came to all the people, and said, "How long will you falter between two opinions? If the Lord is God, follow Him; but if Baal, follow him." But the people answered him not a word. Then Elijah said to the people, "I alone am left a prophet of the Lord; but Baal's prophets are four hundred and fifty men. Therefore let them give us two bulls; and let them choose one bull for themselves, cut it in pieces, and lay it on the wood, but put no fire under it; and I will prepare the other bull, and lay it on the wood, but put no fire under it. Then you call on the name of your gods, and I will call on the name of the Lord; and the God who answers by fire, He is God." So all the people answered and said, "It is well spoken." —1 Kings 18:20-24 (NKJV)

Elijah is self-motivated. He defeats the prophets of Baal on Mount Carmel. There's a place for this type of leader; but Elijah never would have led the Israelites out of Egypt. Why? Because he operated on his own. There is a progression in spiritual maturity: at first, you don't care; then, you need to be guided; later, you're motivated; and, finally, you grow into the final stage.

Leaders

One of the two who heard John speak, and followed Him, was Andrew, Simon Peter's brother. He first found his own brother Simon, and said to him, "We have found the Messiah" (which is translated, the Christ). And he brought him to Jesus.

Now when Jesus looked at him, He said, "You are Simon the son of Jonah. You shall be called Cephas" (which is translated, A Stone). — John 1:40-42 (NKJV)

Andrew was not comfortable meeting Jesus by himself. He brought others in with him. You may have heard the saying, "If you're making progress, but no one is walking behind you, you're not a leader; you're just taking a walk." This rings true. You may be right in your spiritual journey, but if you can't bring a team of others with you, you're not accomplishing in full the thing God has assigned you to do. True maturity and leadership invite others to join the cause. Jesus was the Word of God, and He did everything with His twelve disciples—guys who regularly got on His nerves. He knew He had to bring people with Him.

Think about where you are in your participation journey. Is your default sentiment, "I just don't care"? Or maybe, your response is more along the lines of, "I simply need to be directed." Are you at a place where you primarily get things done by yourself ? Or, perhaps, have you matured to a place in which you can teach others how to get the work done?

We must carefully consider who we bring alongside us. Jesus selected Matthew, a tax collector—an unlikely choice to most onlookers. The Pharisees grew angry with Jesus because He made a regular habit of eating with sinners. Interestingly enough, we see that most of the people Jesus called were individuals who could, in turn, bring in other people to the cause.

Your team will often be comprised of some level of a mixed multitude; especially if you are a church leader. Some will never care. As a leader, be at peace with that. Some will never do the work without accountability. Accept this fact and embrace them. Some people want to get work done; give them a cubicle and an assignment. Then, there's the last group, in which we all want to be: the true leaders. They catch the vision, see the vision, go to work, and bring others with them.

CLOSING THOUGHTS

Moving from taker to giver, from wanderer to leader, is a lifelong process. Our purpose in outlining the categories of people is not to make anyone feel inadequate, but rather to encourage you to become all that God has intended and desired for you. Our maturity and leadership skills reach their zenith only when we surrender to God, and admit that we cannot achieve anything on our own.

As you examine yourself and your team, be honest about what you find. The only way to move forward is to be clear about where you are today. There is a time to take, and a time to give. There is a time to follow, and a time to lead. Let the Holy Spirit guide you and your team as you pursue Him, and work to accomplish the vision He's given you. My prayers are with you as you pursue becoming the leader that God has created you to be.

Dr. Derek Grier is the founding pastor of Grace Church in Dumfries, Virginia. He was ordained as a bishop in 2008 and earned a Master's in Education from Regent University and a Doctorate in Practical Ministry from Wagner University. Dr Grier has authored several books, and leads programs specializing in education, training, and outreach. Derek and his wife, Yeromitou, live in northern Virginia and have two adult sons

CPSIA information can be obtained
at www.ICGtesting.com
Printed in the USA
FFHW021736240319
51198508-56679FF